The Family Life of a Christian Leader

The Family Life of a
Christian Leader

Ajith Fernando

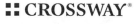

WHEATON, ILLINOIS

Library of Congress Cataloging-in-Publication Data

Names: Fernando, Ajith, author.
Title: The family life of a Christian leader / Ajith Fernando.
Description: Wheaton : Crossway, 2016.
Identifiers: LCCN 2015046436 (print) | LCCN 2016013212 (ebook) | ISBN 9781433552908 (tp) | ISBN 9781433552939 (epub) | ISBN 9781433552915 (pdf) | ISBN 9781433552922 (mobi)
Subjects: LCSH: Christian life. | Christian leadership. | Families—Religious life.
Classification: LCC BV4501.3 .F474 2016 (print) | LCC BV4501.3 (ebook) | DDC 253/.22—dc23
LC record available at http://lccn.loc.gov/2015046436

Crossway is a publishing ministry of Good News Publishers.

VP		26	25	24	23	22	21	20	19	18	17	16
15	14	13	12	11	10	9	8	7	6	5	4	3	2	1

To my dear friends
Lokki and Mohini Abhayaratne
Anbahan and Sylvanthi Ariyadorai
Timothy and Surendrani de Alwis
Ceraman and Sureshini Moses
Emmanuel and Sugantha Gunaratnam
Austen and Radhika Mascranghe
Douglas and Shiranthi Ponniah
Andrew and Rhoda Sunder Singh
whose marriages have stood the test

Contents

Rule #3: Do Not Let the Sun Go Down on Anger
Rule #4: Give No Opportunity to the Devil
The Aim Is Unity, Not Victory
Apologizing
God Is There

Children Are a Blessing
Let Them Know That They Are a Delight to You
    Delighting in Children
    Desiring to Help
    When We Cannot Be There for Them
    Keeping Promises
    Spending Time with Our Children
A Word to Parents Who Have Not Experienced Delight

Children and Youth Like to Have Fun
    Fun-Friendly Families
    The Commercialization and Competitiveness of Fun
    Television and the Cyber World
Traditions and Celebrations
Nurturing Secure Children
    A Mother's Love Protects the Children
    Incomplete Attention Can Harm Children
    Parents' Love Combats Comparison

Introduce Them to God's Holiness
Heed Paul's Advice
    Do Not Provoke
    Discipline Lovingly
    Instruct Knowledgeably
    Nourish

Preface

Most of my books have come directly out of my ministry and my attempts to respond biblically to the challenges I've faced in ministry. That is true of this book also. In the past few years, I have been spending lots of time counseling couples before and after marriage, most of whom are involved in ministry in a full-time or volunteer capacity. I also mentor several Christian leaders and pastors who have shared with me about their family life.

My thirty-nine years of marriage have also taught me a lot. In Sri Lanka, student drivers need to have a prominent board with the letter L (for "Learner") attached to the front and back of the vehicles they are driving until they get their licenses. I need to say that after thirty-nine years, I am still driving my marriage vehicle with an L-board. Many of the things about which I write here I learned through mistakes I made. Some of those things will be lifelong struggles, to which we apply God's sufficient grace. I am so grateful that God gave me a patient wife who has accepted me with all my weaknesses. She is the primary human reason we have an enjoyable life as a family. I believe one reason why God gave us a happy family life is so that we can help families who are struggling. But our happiness also was won through struggle—struggle that was accompanied by God's grace.

For many years, I have been teaching, mainly Christian leaders, on biblical principles that undergird a Christian home; principles such as the priority of God, love, joy, and unity. However, in my personal ministry, I have encountered serious challenges to what I have taught. For instance, I have seen very unhappy families where the parents seem to be very committed to God and to biblical principles. I have had to grapple with these anomalies and see how we could respond to them biblically.

So you will see that after a discussion on a major affirmation about family life, I have inserted a discussion that reflects biblically and practically how to respond to challenges to that affirmation. Following the chapter on God, there is a chapter on crucifying self. Our discussion on love includes discussions on complexities of loving. The discussion of sex includes discussions relating to sexual problems. We have a chapter on disappointment and pain after the chapter on joy, and a chapter on the love fight after the chapter on unity. There is a call to delight in children and another call to discipline children.

This book seeks to be solidly biblical while being specific in applying Scripture to concrete situations in the home. You will see that I don't deal only with texts in the Bible that specifically address family-related issues; rather, I take basic biblical principles of behavior and seek to apply those to family life. This buttresses the conviction that if we practice biblical Christianity in a thoroughgoing way in the home, we will arrive at God's beautiful plan for a loving, joyous, and holy home.

I want to thank those who have shared their life journeys with me and helped me sharpen my understanding of the dynamics of Christian living. I also want to thank the many pastors and Christian leaders who have urged me to put into writing the material they were introduced to in seminars I have led on the topic of family. Special thanks go to Youth for Christ board member Andrew Sunder Singh, who kept bugging me about the need to write a book like this. I also want to express my gratitude to my wife, Nelun, and children, Nirmali and Asiri, who have taught me more about family life than anyone else. They demonstrated the biblical practice of patience with a husband and father with so many weaknesses. I have consulted my wife more on this book than on any other I have written, and her perspective has added much richness to these pages. I also want to thank my father and mother, who demonstrated that two highly incompatible people who refuse to give up on each other can give their children a happy and secure home in which to grow up in every way, especially in the ways of God. So much of who their five children are (all believers with hearts for service) has been mediated through their influence upon our lives.

When I started preparing the series of talks that ended up in this book, there was no book that was as helpful to me as *God, Marriage, and Family: Rebuilding the Biblical Foundation* by Andreas J. Köstenberger with David W. Jones.[1] This excellent book gives biblical bases for different aspects of Christian family living. I am surprised and embarrassed that I quote it so little in this book. I think the reason is that I got many biblical principles from it and then pursued my own applications of those principles. Still, I acknowledge my indebtedness to this book. I also wish to place on record my gratitude to Crossway's Greg Bailey for his expert editing of this book.

I am convinced that one of the greatest gifts the church can give to the world today is a healthy and practically fulfilling understanding of family life. But if we are to make this contribution to our nations, we must first get our act together! I pray that this book will serve many by being a source of encouragement to them to follow the biblical way of family living.

1

God

Christian leaders naturally accept that the most important factor in their family life is God; that is, their commitment to God and God's commitment to them. But while we tend to take this for granted, it is necessary for me to say some things about God's role in our family lives right at the start of this book.

God Is Committed to Our Marriages

We often quote Joshua's statement of commitment to serve God with his family: "As for me and my house, we will serve the LORD" (Josh. 24:15). But more important than our decision as families to serve the Lord is God's decision to bless our marriages and families.

About marriage, Jesus said, "What therefore God has joined together, let not man separate" (Matt. 19:6). That statement has become a major proclamation given at Christian wedding services.

When a couple plans a wedding service, they look into many things: Who should be invited? What should they wear? Who will decorate the church? Who will perform the music, preach the homily, and solemnize the marriage proper? Who will sign as attesting witnesses? Will there be a separate reception or merely some refreshments outside the church after the service? These are important things to think about. However, rarely does the couple think seriously about the vows they will make before God. The vows are viewed as a necessary part of the ritual, but not a part that requires much preparation.

Yet the vows are the key to the marriage. They are part of the covenant that is made that day, a covenant of which God is the primary partner. He comes to bless, seal, and protect the marriage. And Jesus says that because God joins the couple together, no human being or human agency must separate them. This is so even when the persons who have married do not seem to be suited for each other. Once God has joined the couple together, he can provide them with the grace to stay together and develop a good home.

Indeed, the couple may encounter huge problems that seem to be impossible to resolve. But the fact that God has joined them together gives them the confidence that he has the ability to keep them together. They will need to work hard to solve their problems, but they can do so with the confidence that, if they are obedient to God, God will see them through. So they do not talk about getting divorced. Neither one tells a person who is not their spouse, "You are the kind of person I should have married." I have heard of Christians who have told a person of the opposite sex, "My husband/wife does not satisfy me," implying that this other person could give them the satisfaction they miss from their spouses. Such statements have no place in a Christian marriage. These statements are indications that the couple does not believe that God will help them succeed in their marriage.

Belief is one of the basic values of Christianity, and it applies to every area of life. When it comes to marriage, we believe that the God who has sealed our marriage covenants will help us keep our marriages safe and growing until the end. This belief gives us the strength to battle for a happy home without giving up when the problems become huge and complex. Believing Christians re-fuse to yield to the temptation to throw up their hands in despair or self-pity when there is a problem. Trusting in God's ability, they fight the fight of faith for their marriages with humility, knowing that their sinful attitudes can hinder God's healing grace (more on that in the next chapter).

The assurance that the God who is committed to our families is bigger than every problem we face is also a source of great peace and security. The Bible promises that "for those who love God all things work together for good" (Rom. 8:28). This is the assurance with which we face every crisis that our marriages and families encounter. We believe God can turn a crisis into something good.

At the start of our marriage, my wife and I decided that, in keeping with Paul's instruction, "Do not let the sun go down on your anger" (Eph. 4:26), when we have a disagreement, we will not go to sleep until it is solved and unity is restored. My wife and I have such different personalities that we took some years to adjust to each other. So in those first few years, we had many "love fights" that extended late into the night until a resolution came. I learned an important lesson during that time. With my mouth, I spoke to my wife, and with my ears, I listened to her. But in my heart, I prayed to God. My prayer was usually something like this: "Please! Oh, please, God, help us!"

The knowledge that God was involved in our issues changed our whole perspective on them. Deep down, we experienced that "peace of God, which surpasses all understanding" (Phil. 4:7) that comes as a result of letting our "requests be made known to God" (v. 6). That peace rules in our hearts (Col. 3:15). As such, it moderates our arguments. How can we say unkind things to our spouses and children or use obscene language when God is right there as part of the conversation? Why should we panic when we have the peace of realizing that God is there to see us through to a resolution? Knowing that God is committed to our marriages markedly influences our attitude to the problems we face.

Work for All in the Family to Be Committed to God

It goes without saying that the greatest desire of Christian leaders for the members of our families is that they become God's children and follow him. God's desire for Israel is surely our desire for our families: "Oh that they had such a heart as this always, to fear me and to keep all my commandments, that it might go well with them and with their descendants forever!" (Deut. 5:29).

I am not going to spend much time with the fact that it is absolutely essential for a committed Christian to marry a committed Christian. The strong denunciation in Ezra 9 and 10 of the practice of marrying those who do not follow God serves as a serious warning against considering such a step. Yet, sadly, many Christians have done this. The force of love or parental pressure was so irresistible that they chose to disobey God and marry unbelievers. Thankfully, God does not abandon those who repent of wrong decisions they have made. Paul teaches that a person married to an unbeliever should remain faithful to him or her (1 Cor. 7:12–13). He even says that, because of the believer, the unbelieving spouse is, in a sense, made holy, thus making the children born to that marriage holy (v. 14).

What can we do to encourage the members of our families to follow God? Let me mention two powerful actions we can take.

The Power of a Beautiful Life

Peter shows how important it is for Christians to work toward bringing their unbelieving spouses to Christ. He implies that the beauty of their lives rather than their words is most powerful in challenging unbelieving spouses. He says, "Likewise, wives, be subject to your own husbands, so that even if some do not obey the word, they may be won without a word by the conduct of their wives, when they see your respectful and pure conduct" (1 Pet. 3:1–2). He goes on to show the power of a beautiful life: "Let your adorning be the hidden person of the heart with the imperishable beauty of a gentle and quiet spirit, which in God's sight is very precious" (v. 4). Today there is a lot of emphasis on people being beautiful when they are outside their homes. Peter is teaching here that being beautiful to our spouses in the way we behave is far more important. Song of Solomon does commend outward physical beauty. However, there the husband and wife are beautiful for each other, not for the world outside to see. How countercultural is the biblical approach to family! We aim to be beautiful primarily in order to bring joy to our spouses!

The evangelist Rodney "Gypsy" Smith (1860–1947) served for a time with the Wesleyan mission in Manchester, England. One of the women in that ministry frequently requested prayers for the conversion of her husband, John. Sadly, she also had a terrible temper. Sometimes when her husband would be close to surrendering to the claims of Christ, she would upset him by having a temper tantrum. Her husband would say, "Well, Mary, if that is religion, I don't want it." She would later apologize and ask his forgiveness, but he made a habit of using her temper as his reason for not following Christ.

One day, Smith talked to the woman frankly and told her that she must learn to overcome her temper. He assured her that Christ would give her the grace to enable her to curb her habit. Believing in God, she made a commitment to start a new chapter in her life. It happened to be at a time when they were fixing up their house. Mary had just put in new carpet and a new ceiling lamp, which she had hung in the hallway. John, not knowing about the new lamp, came home carrying something on his shoulder. As he turned the corner, he hit the lamp, and it all came crashing down in shattered pieces.

John braced for his wife's usual response, a torrent of angry words and berating comments. But rather than the typical response, John was surprised to hear nothing. Instead, his wife looked down over the stairs at him and simply said: "Never mind, husband! It is all right; we can get another lamp." Confused and surprised, John looked up at her.

"Mary, what's the matter?"

She calmly replied, "O, my dear, I have trusted Jesus to cure me of my temper."

John, still amazed at his wife's unexpected response, said: "Well, if he has cured you, come right down and pray for me, for that's what I want. If there is enough in religion to cure your temper, I want the same religion." After years of prayers, John was converted that very day.[1]

Later we will see how important words are within the home, but without the beauty of a loving life, words are powerless. How many stories there are of rebellious children who, unable to shake off the loving example of their mothers' lives, finally yielded to Christ.

The Power of Prayer

Along with a beautiful life, prayer also goes a long way in bringing salvation to family members. Epaphras was probably the one who took the gospel to Colossae (Col. 1:7). He was with Paul when the apostle wrote his letter to the Colossian church. Of him, Paul writes, "Epaphras, who is one of you, a servant of Christ Jesus, greets you, always struggling on your behalf in his prayers, that you may stand mature and fully assured in all the will of God" (Col. 4:12). This spiritual father was struggling or "wrestling" (NIV) in prayer on behalf of his fellow Colossian believers while he was separated from them. Likewise, shortly after expressing deep sorrow over the fact that his own people, the Jews, had not accepted Christ's salvation (Rom. 9:1–3), Paul says, "Brothers, my heart's desire and prayer to God for them is that they may be saved" (10:1). Whatever one's theology of election is, we must accept that God uses prayer as a means of bringing people to salvation.

Often there is a huge battle going on for the souls of our family members. Though sometimes we cannot talk to them about God, we can talk to God about them. Augustine Aurelius (354–430), bishop of Hippo in North Africa, was one of the most influential theologians in the history of the church. He was deeply influenced by the piety and example of his mother, Monica, who was a Christian. But that was not sufficient to lead to his conversion to Christ or to prevent him from living an immoral life. It was only at the age of thirty-three that he finally yielded to Christ. In his autobiographical *Confessions*, he speaks glowingly of the influence his mother's prayers had in his conversion. Interestingly, it was not only her prayers, but also her exemplary life and her persistent pleas for him to change his ways that had a deep influence upon him. Her work on earth complete, she died a few days after his conversion.

The name Scudder is an important one in South Asian mission studies. Dr. John Scudder came from America to Sri Lanka as a missionary and then went to India. All of his seven children became missionaries. John said that his seven children were prayed into the kingdom by their mother, Harriet. She had the habit of spending the birthdays of each of her children fasting and praying for that child. John and Harriet's granddaughter, Ida Scudder (1870–1959), founded the famous Vellore Medical College and hospital in Tamil Nadu, South India.

Every Christian parent needs to develop a way to pray for his or her children. I mention "a way" because such things can slip from our minds and we can forget to pray. So we need to develop disciplines that ensure that we pray for our children. When parents pray together, prayer for their children should surely be an indispensable ingredient of that prayer time. Paul mentions praying for the recipients of ten of his thirteen letters. But for his spiritual child, Timothy, he says that he prayed "night and day" (2 Tim. 1:3). Our physical children and our spouses, as well as our spiritual children, should occupy central places in our prayer lives. We should be praying for them daily, perhaps many times a day. When our children have left home, one of the ways we can fulfill our parenting responsibilities is by praying for them. We can follow their schedules with our prayers and bring up their needs. And if they are not yet converted, we can pray for their salvation.

In chapter 13, I will discuss the important part that instruction in the Word has in the lives of children.

God First

Jesus's statement, "But seek first the kingdom of God and his righteousness, and all these things will be added to you" (Matt. 6:33), applies to all Christians, including leaders. The principle behind Paul's advice to children relating to the care of aged parents—"Let them first learn to show godliness to their own household" (1 Tim. 5:4)—relates to parents too. When leaders practice Christianity in their homes, this brings credibility to their leadership and ministry. We urge our family members to be totally committed to God, and those we minister among see this. In his famous speech to Israel, like a good leader, Joshua urged the people to total dedication to God: "Now therefore fear the LORD and serve him in sincerity and in faithfulness. Put away the gods that your fathers served beyond the River and in Egypt, and serve the LORD" (Josh. 24:14). He buttressed that challenge by stating his own commitment to do the same along with his family: "But as for me and my house, we will serve the LORD" (v. 15).

Yet leaders are not immune to the temptation to make decisions for the family that are influenced by the world's standards and that violate God's will. How easy it is for us to ignore the fact that, if we follow God's way, he will provide everything we need for the best life possible. We can have ambitions for ourselves and our children that take us and them backward spiritually. Under the influence of desires for earthly success, we can forget Jesus's questions: "For what will it profit a man if he gains the whole world and forfeits his soul? Or what shall a man give in return for his soul?" (Matt. 16:26).

We cannot assume that leaders will automatically practice Christianity with their families. Let me mention a few examples that highlight some of the challenges leaders face.

When a son is studying for an exam and needs some special instruction, the parents don't mind sending him for a class that clashes with worship services on Sunday—the Lord's Day. They might stop the son from going to the youth fellowship at church because he has to study. Indeed, when the exam is close, he may miss youth fellowship meetings while continuing to go for worship on Sunday. But this neglect of much-needed fellowship sometimes takes place long before the exam time. The child gets the impression that studies are more important than spiritual health. D. L. Moody says: "I would rather, if I went tonight, leave my children in the hope of Christ than leave them millions of money. It seems to me as if we were too ambitious to have them make a name, instead of to train them up for the life they are to lead forever."[2]

Let's take an example from the Christian discipline of giving. A young couple is planning to buy a house. They have saved money for several years to do so. They discover a house that is just the kind of place they want to have as their home. They calculate how they will pay back the loan they will have to take in order to buy this house. They realize that they will be able to make the payments only if they reduce their giving to God's work and to the poor. There is their tithe, which would usually be considered a non-negotiable commitment. There is a child from a poor home, for whose education they had decided to give a substantial monthly payment. Are they going to give up this dream house by continuing with their giving? As giving is part of a Christian's basic non-negotiable expenditure, this couple decides to forgo what looked like a beautiful opportunity.

Some of the most enjoyable television programs are during the times the children are at home, which could be good family times. Prime-time television can be during prime family time. It is nice for family members to watch good television programs (I personally relish an opportunity to watch a good cricket match or a detective program), but it is very important for a family to establish that watching a favorite program is of secondary importance. It must not get in the way of family prayers and other important activities, such as meetings at church or meetings of the small group to which the family belongs. Parents may be forced into missing an important game that is being broadcast on TV because they have to visit a needy person in the hospital. Sometimes a visitor comes right in the middle of an exciting episode of a favorite program. The parents decide to turn off the TV. When the children see their parents making such sacrifices, they get the message about what is important in their home.

If we forget that the work of Christ broke human barriers, we can deny the great biblical teaching of equality by preventing our children from having friendships with people we consider to be of a lower class then ourselves. Moody tells a sad story that a lady told him about her only son. The boy was involved in the evangelistic work of the Young Men's Christian Association (YMCA) and would go out in the streets to distribute tracts. The mother was ambitious that he should make a name for himself and wanted him to make connections with people in high society. She thought it was below his dignity to associate with the poor youth of the YMCA. She wanted him to stop going there, but he did not give up. So she packed him off to a boarding school. From there, he went to a prestigious university, Yale, where he lost his faith.

When she realized this, she wrote to him often, trying to summon him back to the faith. But it was to no avail. The parents did not hear from him for two years. Then they heard that he was in Chicago. After resuming contact with him, the father gave him a large sum of money to start a business. They thought that this would change him, but it didn't. The last they heard of him was that he had drowned in Lake Michigan. What remorse that mother had; but it was too late![3]

Parents make a similar mistake when they object to their son's choice of a partner in life because she comes from a family that is considered socially inferior to them. She is a fine Christian and is suitable for him in every other way. But bondage to social status has blinded the family from seeing a key biblical principle. The decision to oppose that principle gives the message that social status is more important to this family than God and his principles.

Prayer

One of the most obvious signs of the primacy of God in the Christian home is prayer. Yet prayer usually does not happen naturally. We must make it happen. I had wanted to write "Take time to pray" here; instead, I am saying, "Make time to pray." We must proactively pursue the priority of prayer in the home and somehow make the time for it.

The most basic type of prayer in a home is individual prayer in private. This is the context Jesus used when he wanted to teach about genuine prayer. He said, "When you pray, go into your room and shut the door and pray to your Father who is in secret" (Matt. 6:6). During this time, we pray for our family members, as I have mentioned above. The habit of individuals being alone and praying to God is a signature of a Christian home. When I was a child attending a Bible camp with my family, I heard Herbert Epp speaking about his father, Theodore Epp, the founder of the Back to the Bible Broadcast. He said that there were times when his father would be in his room with the door closed. The children knew that he should not be disturbed during these times because he was praying. I have a similar memory of my mother and grandmother. When I went to stay at the home of my grandparents, sometimes I would need to use the restroom early in the morning before dawn. I had to go through my grandparents' room, and I would see my grandmother kneeling in prayer beside her bed with her head covered. It was the same with my mother, whom I would see on her knees every morning.

I believe praying is the most important thing we do on earth. Our children recognize this when they observe the seriousness with which we approach the task of praying. This encourages them to respect and honor God.

Mothers with little children often struggle to make time for concentrated periods of prayer. They need to use their creativity to find suitable times. I once asked a young friend who had two little children how his wife was finding time to pray. He told me that when the children fell asleep in the afternoon, she would immediately pounce on the opportunity to have her time alone with God.

A lady was impressed that her neighbor, who was the mother of many children, seemed to have a demeanor that suggested that she was in intimate contact with God. She asked the mother how she was able to achieve this. The lady pointed to a large apron she always wore. She said that when she sat on a certain chair and put the apron over her head, the children knew that this meant she was praying. There was a rule in the house that the children must be quiet during these times.

Children must know that their parents devote time to prayer because God is important to them. Unconsciously they imbibe the idea that personal prayer is an important aspect of life. This becomes an incentive for them also to become people of prayer. Once "Jesus was praying in a certain place, and when he finished, one of his disciples said to him, 'Lord, teach us to pray, as John taught his disciples'" (Luke 11:1). That question prompted Jesus to give them the Lord's Prayer (vv. 2–4). Seeing Jesus pray gave the disciples a desire to become people of prayer.

The first fourteen chapters of Acts give us a glimpse of the life of the early church. There are twenty-two references to prayer in this section, and most of those are instances of corporate prayer. If corporate prayer is so important to church life, it must surely be important in the most basic unit of the church—the family. The habit of couples praying together regularly and parents praying with their children is an important aspect of the identity and stability of the family. We should also pray together at important family events and when the family faces challenges. The family should recognize that prayer is not just a ritual that is performed at birthdays; rather, it is an important aspect of the celebration. Praying before the start of a long journey or before a family member leaves for an important event helps mediate God's blessings for the journey or the event. It also establishes that God is the One from whom we get our help at important times.

My son played cricket at school when he was in his early teens. We had a habit of praying with him before he left for a game. One day, I was driving him to a game, but I had forgotten to pray with him. While I was driving, he asked me, "Can you pray for me?" He had come to accept that committing a game to the Lord was an important part of his life.

When children grow up, they will not forget that their identity and security as children were wrapped up in praying to God. Sometimes, when they go through a rebellious stage and are tempted to give up the faith, the pleasant memories of these moments with God as a family may make it difficult for them to abandon the faith of their childhood. Even if they do abandon it for a time, these memories could trigger a return to God. I am sure you know of children who have turned their backs on God but who nevertheless ask their parents to pray when they have a special need.

It goes without saying that family prayer should not be legalistic, burdensome, or boring. Parents must do all they can to use their creativity to make it interesting and pleasant: one of those happy things parents and children do as a family. We should try to develop ways for the children to be meaningfully involved during the prayer time. When our children were young, we would first discuss things about which we should pray. Then I would ask, "Who's praying for what?" That became a source of laughter in the home, but also a practice that helped involve the children in the prayer time. Of course, the children's needs have an important place in this prayer time. The fact that they know they can bring those needs to the family and pray about them becomes a major source of security for them.

Again, let me say that, no matter how interesting we make the family prayer time, it is not natural for families to meet regularly for prayer. It is best that one person takes upon himself or herself the responsibility to ensure that the meeting takes place. When the children are young the father or the mother could take on this role. As the children get older, one of them could be given this responsibility. This principle is also important for couples with no children or whose children have left home. It is sad that many Christian couples today do not have a regular time of prayer together. This must change! Either the husband or the wife should ensure that they have such a time.

Conclusion

The main point of this chapter has been that God's involvement is the most important factor in our marriages and families. He is the committed senior partner in the marriage covenant, who helps us fulfill the covenant conditions and works in every situation for our good. On our part, we must be committed to God and to his principles. Failure to be so committed will take us along destructive paths. At a time when families are under attack, when the media and many segments of the culture seem to be at war against the biblical understanding of marriage and family, Christians must remain enthusiastic about these God-created institutions.

2

Crucifying Self

In the last chapter, we said that God's commitment and involvement assure committed Christians of joyous and fulfilling marriages and families. Why, then, do so many Christian leaders have unhappy marriages loaded with strife? In this book, I will say many things that provide answers to that question, but I first want to present a practice that is vital to a healthy Christian home. In fact, it is basic to the whole Christian life, but even Christian leaders often stumble in connection with it.

Unwillingness to Crucify Self: A Major Cause of Conflicts

After thirty-nine years of marriage and countless counseling appointments, I have come to realize that what most often takes away the joy and peace of our homes is the refusal to crucify self. This problem is seen in the church too. The real reason for most church conflicts is not the outward issue that the conflict is supposed to be about. These outward issues may be doctrinal, spiritual, strategic, administrative, or related to personnel. But what fuels conflicts most often are bruised and unbending egos.

In a Christian marriage or church, when there is a conflict or disagreement, the end we desire is not victory but unity under the will of God. All parties should battle for God's will, and once that has been found, they should submit to it. But in most conflicts, even though we give lip service to God's will, what we want most is not for Christ to be honored but for our side to win, our power to be exercised, or our authority or influence to prevail. Small people want small victories, and they forget about the greater good in their pursuit of victory. It is easy to let our commitment to ourselves overcomes our sensitivity to God's will so that we don't strive to submit to it. When people feel humiliated because they sense that their power or influence has been reduced, or when they sense that their side in a disagreement has lost, they often forget Christian principles in their reaction to the situation. Their reaction aggravates the problem. To put it in biblical language, they refuse to crucify self.

Crucifying self is one of the most basic practices of the Christian life. It was part of Jesus's primary call to discipleship: "If anyone would come after me, let him deny himself and take up his cross daily and follow me" (Luke 9:23). Denying self and taking up the cross are daily practices for the Christian. Paul appeals to us, "Present your bodies as a living sacrifice, holy and acceptable to God" (Rom. 12:1). In the old sacrificial system, people sacrificed animals. Now we give our own lives,[1] and we do so constantly. As we live, we are dying. This is no mere ritual. It is a case of dying every day. Of himself, Paul says: "I have been crucified with Christ. It is no longer I who live, but Christ who lives in me" (Gal. 2:20). Every day, we are faced with situations in which our wills clash with God's. Knowing that our thinking and ways are so different from God's thinking and ways (Isa. 55:8–9), we should be asking God daily what he wants us to crucify. Our failure to crucify self in the home could lead to an unhappy home.

How Crucifying Self Helps Foster a Healthy Home

Let's look at some examples that show that crucifying self is a key to fostering a healthy home:

- I usually work till late at night, so when I get up in the morning, I feel very groggy. As a true Sri Lankan, I like to have a cup of tea the moment I get up in the morning. My wife is a morning person and gets up much earlier than me. She makes our tea and pours mine into a flask. The first thing I do when I get up is to go to the kitchen to get my cup of tea. What if I find that the tea is not prepared? My first reaction could be to get annoyed. I could express this annoyance with an unnecessary question or accusation, even though I have come to realize that if my wife has not prepared tea, it is usually because she has a good reason. As a Christian, I must crucify my instinctual tendency to express annoyance. A person who had been happily married for fifty years was asked for the secret of his happy marriage. He said that every day there was something he did not say.[2] He was crucifying self daily.
- Men can respond very unreasonably when their wives reject their requests to have sexual intercourse. Later, I will describe how important sexual intercourse is for a complete marriage and how men naturally desire this, sometimes more than their wives do. Yet it is wrong for a man to force himself on his wife, even though her rejection is a blow to his ego. It may be quite natural for him to respond angrily and hurt his wife with harsh words or even physical blows. But a biblical husband crucifies that inclination and controls his response. He loves his wife as himself and gives up his plans because of her desires and moods.
- A wife can be hurt by a statement her husband makes in front of her children at the dinner table (a very unwise action by the husband!). She can hit back angrily in front of the children. And he can respond with an angry rejoinder resulting in a Ping-Pong game of attacks and counterattacks at the table. The children are distressed to see their parents fighting in this way. At each step of this game, either the husband or wife can halt the battle by refusing to hit back. They must indeed talk about this thing that

has caused so much unpleasantness, but the dining table is not the place to do so, and the mood of the conversation should not continue. People who lash out when they are angry end up saying unkind things—that is, they become unkind people. A wise Christian decides to crucify his or her natural inclination and postpone the confrontation until the time and place are suitable and the emotions have cooled down to enable sensible conversation.

- As study and preparation have always been challenges for me, I am often at my desk studying and preparing until a few minutes before I leave home for my office or an appointment. Often, I study a few minutes too long. Then I dress as quickly as I can and rush out of the house. During the early years of my marriage, I often forgot to tell my wife that I was going. This was, as I remember, not a problem in the home I grew up in. But that is not how my wife grew up. She was often justifiably quite upset to find that her husband was missing. I had to learn to change my habits and tell her before I left. Sometimes I forgot and left without telling her in spite of my desire to do so. We did not have a phone in those early years. So I had to come back home, say "Goodbye," and resume my journey—a rather inconvenient procedure! I had to crucify my convenience in order to love my wife as I should.

- A father comes home very tired and wants to go to bed early. His daughter is going to a party that evening and asks him whether he could pick her up and bring her home around midnight. His heart groans within him when he hears the request, but he crucifies his desire for sleep and agrees to pick up his daughter. Actually, agreeing to his daughter's request is the best thing the father could do. I have done this often with my children, and I have always been happy that I got a chance to help them in this way. There is something beautiful about little, loving sacrifices made for the ones we love. The greatest wealth of the home is happiness. It is well worth giving up a little sleep in order to gain wealth in this way.

- A mother loves her job and does it well for the glory of God. She also loves the family God gave her. Lately, she has begun to realize that her children are suffering because her job prevents her from giving them the time they require. To take a few years off from her profession would seem to be suicidal in terms of professional advancement. But she decides to do it by crucifying her desire for the joy she finds in her profession and her legitimate goal of advancing in her career.

- A wonderful opportunity comes to a husband to go for three months of training abroad. It would greatly help him advance in his career and in the work that he loves and does for the glory of God. But two weeks before he is to leave, his wife contracts a viral infection that leaves her very weak. The doctor says that it will take several weeks for her to regain her strength. The husband realizes that his wife would find it very difficult to run the home without him. He crucifies his desire to get training in order to be able to help his wife. Someone else goes for the training.

- A couple is having a debate over a conflict that has arisen in their relationship. As they proceed, it soon becomes clear that both have made mistakes that have contributed to the conflict. The Christian thing would be for both of them to apologize for the wrongs they have done. But to do so would be humiliating and would seem like conceding victory to the other. One of them needs to crucify self, be humble, and apologize first. Usually after that, the other one also apologizes. Later we will show that those who do not apologize are weak people. Our greatest strength in life is being undergirded by grace. The failure to apologize hinders grace from coming into our lives. That, in turn, makes us weak people, without the joy of living under grace.

- A wife did something very bad. She confessed her sin and received forgiveness from God and from her husband.

They started over with their relationship on the firm footing of grace. But now, several months later, they are facing a conflict and are in a heated debate. The husband knows that if he brings up his wife's past sin, he could score a strong point over her. But just as God forgives and forgets our sins (Jer. 31:34), Christians who have forgiven the sins done against them must behave as if they have forgotten those sins. The husband crucifies self by resisting the temptation to bring up this issue in the debate.

- A husband finds himself straying to unedifying websites and finding sexual gratification from what he sees. This could ruin his relationship with his wife and result in her becoming sexually unattractive to him because of the false and satisfaction-destroying world of sex presented on the Internet. He has to decide to crucify his desire to see unedifying imagery (not only on the Internet, but also on TV and even on billboards) in order to love God and his wife. Because the Internet can be such a trap, I have found having strong Internet-blocking and accountability software very helpful. One of my accountability partners gets a weekly report on my Internet watching through Covenant Eyes, the software program I use.

- A Christian woman has developed a very productive and warm working relationship with a male colleague alongside whom she works. As they are together a lot, they chat about many things, and an uncanny sense of understanding of each other's way of thinking seems to have developed. They enjoy being with each other and find themselves naturally getting next to each other at lunch and at other times. Soon she finds that she is beginning to desire to be with him and tell him personal things about her life. She senses that she is reluctant to tell her husband about all the details of her relationship with this man. That, of course, is a sign of grave danger. It is certainly natural for Christians to find some members of the opposite sex more attractive than others. It is not wrong to like such people. But it is easy to cross the line and develop an inappropriate relationship with such a person. A biblical Christian crucifies the desire to be with such a person all the time and chooses to forgo the pleasure of his or her company. By the way, social media such as Facebook are fostering many such inappropriate relationships these days. More on that later.

- A husband is having a very stressful time at work. He is very busy and not getting the sleep that he needs. Consequently, he is very irritable and is easily annoyed, especially at home. He recognizes that this problem is because of his stress. This makes him alert to the possibility of doing something unkind. So when he is tempted to snap at his wife or children, he consciously crucifies that desire and chooses not to give expression to his instinctual reaction. Actually, when my children were small, I found it helpful to tell them that I was under stress so that they would know that they were not the cause of my irritability.
- A mother has decided what kind of wife her son will get. She has a list of the qualities that her son's bride must have. Her son falls in love with a wonderful Christian girl, but she doesn't meet some of his mother's requirements. She is too dark skinned; her figure is such that the mother would not classify her as physically beautiful; her parents are from a much poorer family than theirs; and she falls far short of the educational qualifications she wanted for her son's wife. She is also upset that she was not actively involved in her son's crucial decision to love his girl. What will she do? There are no biblical reasons for rejecting her son's choice. She has to crucify her desires so that her son can be happily married to this good girl.

Our refusal to crucify self is a sign of personal weakness. People like to cling to their ideas and are afraid to give in to others for the greater good. They see it as a sign of failure. Such fear of this kind of "failure" is a sign of insecurity. Sadly, by their stubbornness, they hurt others. Their spouses and children end up bruised by their refusal to surrender their will for the greater good. They may be "righteous" people, but they have become unkind. Children who hurt their parents by their angry insistence on getting their way must realize that they too have become unkind. Husbands who say hurtful things to their wives when they are irritated have also become unkind. That must stop!

Christians don't hurt people! They have to learn that by doing so, they are displeasing God and doing great damage to themselves and others. Ultimately, it is an issue of whether we love God and our family members enough to surrender our wills and forgo some things that we don't want to give up. Sometimes Christians who have very strong convictions find it difficult to do this. They may be prominent Christian leaders, but they are unholy people. They shouldn't be leaders in the church.

Help Is Available

Yet I must make clear that crucifying the flesh is not something we do in our own strength. God provides the grace for us to do it. One way he does this is by giving us friends to help us in our times of need. Accountability partners can help us by monitoring our behavior in our weak areas, such as excessive anger and unhealthy Internet watching. Respected friends and leaders can counsel us. Perceptive listeners are able to see the root causes for family disharmony that those embroiled in the problem don't see. When things look very gloomy, others can help us see things in a different light and open ways for us to work toward effective solutions.

I have worked with couples who thought they were going through problems that were impossible to solve. Just the intervention of another who gives them the opportunity to listen to each other and understand each other's behaviors can result in dramatic changes for good in their relationship. This is particularly helpful in the early years of marriage, when one spouse may be hurt by the other's actions. He or she thinks the spouse is being unkind, when the real issue is something connected to the spouse's personality or the way the spouse grew up (that is, his or her background).

But more important, God helps us by giving us the ability and the strength to crucify the flesh. Paul says, "*By the Spirit* you put to death the deeds of the body" (Rom. 8:13). The Spirit is there to enable us to do this. We must accept that we have problems. We must pray, asking God to help us. God can break through with his solutions, but on our part, there must be a willingness to crucify self. He gives us the strength to do that. God can work marvelously with people who are willing to change in order for him to do what he wishes with them.

Sometimes the issue is more complex than simply needing to crucify self. There may be other factors that can trigger reactions like those described above. Unhealed wounds from hurts received earlier in life can result in a person reacting excessively to disagreeable experiences. For example, people who were mercilessly punished and hurt as children can be wary about giving in during a conflict, given the way others exploited situations and hurt them during their childhoods. Guilt over sins committed before or during marriage can result in people having difficulty loving themselves, which results in them being hostile toward others in the family who try to love them. Some children grew up as "spoiled brats" who got most of what they asked for if they cried loudly enough. As adults, these people find it difficult to give up their desires for the benefit of others, as they are not skilled in living with unfulfilled desires. We will deal with these issues later in the book. But even for people facing such handicaps, the grace of God is sufficient to heal and enable godly behavior.

Believe That God's Will Is Perfect

A key factor to consider is what the Bible says about the fruit of crucifying self. Immediately after giving his call to deny self and take up the cross, Jesus said, "For whoever would save his life will lose it, but whoever loses his life for my sake will save it" (Luke 9:24). Denying self in obedience to Christ is not something that will harm us. It is the pathway to life. It is the best thing that we can do for our progress and joy in life. Paul says that when we "present [our] bodies as a living sacrifice," we "discern" that "the will of God" is "good and acceptable and perfect" (Rom. 12:1–2). We must believe this—that God's will is perfect. If we do, we will take the risk of denying self, accepting that we did wrong and apologizing, knowing that God will look after us because of that step of obedience.

Yes, we may have had unpleasant and hurtful experiences related to giving things up. But when God asks us to do something, it is only because it is the best thing for us. So when we deny self, we do so believing that God's will is best for us. If we do not believe God, then whether we deny self or not, we will lose our peace and joy. Paul says that the "God of hope [will] fill you with all joy and peace *in believing*" (Rom. 15:13). As in everything in the Christian life, belief is the pathway to victory. We believe in the goodness of God's will and make decisions that seem like sacrifices, only to find that they are the pathway to blessing.

If we are causing hurt and unhappiness in our family life because of some problem on our part, we must regard it as an urgent matter that requires immediate attention. We cannot afford to compromise here. It is foolish to do so because we end up hurting ourselves and our loved ones. But more seriously, this is rebellion against God—a very dangerous and stupid thing to do. We should do all we can and seek all the help we can get to overcome this problem.

Conclusion

Just as salvation is a gift of grace, so is sanctification. God is there to help those who are willing to let his will be uppermost in their lives. And in family life, as in every other aspect of life, when our will clashes with God's will, we must crucify the flesh.

3

Love

In the Bible, love is presented as a key Christian value. Paul describes it as the most important characteristic of Christian behavior (1 Cor. 13:1–3, 13). If so, love must be a key value of the Christian home too. It is significant that the primary advice given to husbands regarding marriage in the New Testament is for them to love their wives (Eph. 5:25, 28, 33; Col. 3:19). There is a common idea among people in Sri Lanka that a couple should enjoy as much as they can before marriage because, after that, their relationship is going to turn sour and the spark of love will grow dim. We strongly disagree! We affirm that Christian love practiced in the home results in a joyous marriage where the love remains fresh all through life on earth. In this and the next chapter, we will explore the implications of seeing love as a primary characteristic of a Christian home.

Love as an End in Itself[1]

Paul urges the Corinthians to "Pursue love" (1 Cor. 14:1). The Greek verb translated as "pursue" (*diōkō*) is a strong word meaning "to pursue, chase, or hunt." *The Revised Standard Version* translates this part of the verse, "Make love your aim." Loving

41

is a major ambition in the life of a Christian. It is something we pursue. That is our approach to life in the family. We look for opportunities to love our family members.

The approach of many to family relationships could be called one of concession. People approach situations with these types of attitudes: "I will go this far and no further"; "Somehow I must get him to agree to this, and I will use my persuasive skills to achieve that"; or, "OK, I will agree to this unhappily, just to keep her quiet." Getting something from another is viewed as a victory over that person. Giving something to the other is viewed as a concession. In a truly Christian home, there are no winners and losers. We have won if we are wholeheartedly agreed upon something, if we have expressed love for each other. So we ask these types of questions: "How can I reduce her load of work?" "What can I do to bring joy to him today?" or, "How can I show her that I enjoy being close to her?" Loving our family members is our ambition in life, our measure of success.

A key aspect of the biblical understanding is that love is an end in itself, not simply a means to an end. That is, when we have loved, we have achieved our goal (as 1 Cor. 14:1 says); we have been successful. We do not love in order to get something for ourselves; when we have loved, we have received all we wanted: to be loving people. Loving is our lifestyle, our way of living, our desire. We are happy just to love, and the results we get are of secondary importance.

The concession approach to family relationships reaches its fullest expression with the strategy of bargaining, which is seen in novels and the media. It has even been advocated in popular books as a fitting way to be fulfilled in relationships. In this approach, one manipulates the other with expressions of love, putting the other person in a mood to give what one wants. Delilah did this with Samson. But often it is more subtle than Delilah's inflaming of Samson's lust. A man can give flowers to his wife in order to put her in a good mood so that she will agree to something. Or he can give flowers simply as an expression of his love for her. A woman can let her husband watch a key football game on TV during a busy time at home because she wants to prepare him for a request she will make for some new clothes. Or she can release him to watch it simply because she loves him and is happy to see him enjoying what he likes.

In a loving home, there is a kind of partnership of love that is forged out of many experiences of love freely, sacrificially, and joyfully given. Loving acts are not concessions that are reluctantly made, but gifts that are happily given. We follow a Master who asked us to go a second mile when compelled to carry a burden for one mile (Matt. 5:41). No "Work to rule" here! Rather, it is: "Delighted to serve." For instance, the wife usually washes the dishes at night. One evening, after dinner, she is on a long phone call with her mother. Her husband sacrifices a good program on TV and washes the dishes while she is on the phone—not reluctantly, but happily, as an expression of love. Or a son comes home and finds his mother in bed with a headache. The dinner is not prepared. The son immediately goes about the business of preparing the dinner, even though he is not fond of cooking.

Such attitudes and actions markedly influence the atmosphere of the home. There is brightness and joy when members know that each is committed to the welfare and joy of the others. When a family member, who is usually very considerate, slips up and does not do his or her job, that lapse is not devastating. The others at home know that the offender is committed to their welfare and that such lapses are not the usual pattern. Of a loving wife and mother, Proverbs says, "Her children rise up and call her blessed; her husband also, and he praises her" (31:28). There is appreciation in a home where love is freely given.

I always try to read the inscriptions pasted on the backs of the three-wheel scooter taxis that are a common mode of transport in Sri Lanka. Some are religious, such as, "Praise the Lord" or "The Buddha's way; the path to freedom." Some are proverbs, like the very common, "He who climbs not high, falls not low" (an approach I do not subscribe to!). But in my nonscientific survey, the most popular topic I have found is the scooter owners' mothers. The stickers are mostly statements of gratitude for them. The taxi drivers know that no one cared for them as lovingly and sacrificially as their mothers. So when they want to express something that will stamp the character of their vehicle, they choose to say something about their mothers. One could wish there were such warm feelings about all the members of the family.

It Is Difficult to Show Love to People Who Are Not Content

If one member is always willing to love the other sacrificially while that other is always trying to grab whatever he or she can get from the first, then the Christian model of love faces severe challenges. When grabbing people get what they want, they may be happy for a time, but soon they want more. Such people will never be happy, and their spouses will struggle with frustration in their attempts to be loving.

Sometimes these people are unhappy about things that cannot be changed. A husband cannot simply change his job because there are things about it that his wife does not like. A sick wife cannot make herself well in order to satisfy her husband's sexual demands. A family cannot move to a bigger house in a "better" neighborhood if they do not have the financial resources to make such a change.

Contentment is a key accompaniment to godliness, and Paul says that the combination of the two is a great gain (1 Tim. 6:6). Writing from prison, Paul says, "Not that I am speaking of being in need, for I have learned in whatever situation I am to be content" (Phil. 4:11). John the Baptist told the soldiers who came to him, "Be content with your wages" (Luke 3:14). Hebrews 13:5 gives the key to contentment: "Keep your life free from love of money, and be content with what you have, for he has said, 'I will never leave you nor forsake you.'" We must constantly be aware that we can love the things of the world too much. When we rid ourselves of the love of money, we have taken an important step in the path to a contented life. But this text says that the key is the fact that Jesus is with us. He satisfies our deep yearnings. If he has taken the craving for the world from our lives and filled us with a craving for him, we are contented people. So the next verse says, "So we can confidently say, 'The Lord is my helper; I will not fear; what can man do to me?'" (Heb. 13:6).

Again, writing from prison, Paul speaks of how having Jesus was so much more satisfying than all the earthly honors that he had to give up when he became a Christian. After listing many of those honors, he says: "Indeed, I count everything as loss because of the surpassing worth of knowing Christ Jesus my Lord. For his sake I have suffered the loss of all things and count them as rubbish, in order that I may gain Christ" (Phil. 3:8).

Sadly, I have seen many people who seem to be committed Christians, with an eagerness to serve God, who nevertheless are discontented and unhappy. Consequently, their homes are unhappy places. Are you a happy person; happy in the love of Jesus? Dear reader, Jesus more than satisfies! Learn to lean on him just as a little child leans on his parent. In the security of such a relationship with Christ, you will have inner contentment.

Don't let your personality rob you of the joy of being a contented Christian. Battle for the joy of the Lord! Seek the counsel or help of people you respect and trust to help you come to the place where the love of God breaks through the layers of hurt and pain in your life that prevent you from being a joyful person. Jesus satisfies. With his satisfaction, you will have the strength to face the challenges of deprivation you will experience at home, and you will have the freedom to fully appreciate the love that your spouse shows you. That will bring fulfillment to your spouse and make it so much more joyful for him or her to love you sacrificially.

The path to this freedom of contentment may be a long one. There may be layers of hurt that need to be uncovered and healed before you know real contentment and joy. But the journey is worth taking. This journey is basically an opening of our lives so that we more fully possess the blessings that God has promised in his Word. Thank God there is sufficient grace for this. But we must persevere in opening ourselves to this grace and removing the hindrances to it. Here are some hindrances that I have seen:

- Not fully forgiving someone who has hurt you
- Not being willing to accept that God can turn the unfortunate experiences you have had into something good, so that they no longer should be classified as "unfortunate experiences"
- Letting your life be constantly clouded by the unkind things that people have done to you
- Not crucifying self so that you do not daily open yourself to surrendering something you want to receive or do
- Being ashamed of your past, your physical appearance, your family background, or your lack of educational qualifications. Generally, things people try to hide have a way of having a big influence upon their moods and behavior.
- Refusing to accept your spouse for who he or she is, to be patient with his or her weaknesses and to rejoice in the belief that God will give you a harmonious life despite those weaknesses
- Refusing to believe that God truly wants the best for you and will give the best if you obey him

To have a happy home, you must be a happy person, relishing God's love for you and being content in the fact that he will look after you and give you all that you need for a fulfilled life. And that path to joy is greatly enhanced by a spouse who continues to love the other despite his or her bad moods and discontent. Multiple expressions of love from a loving spouse help break the layers of hurt with which the other has had to contend. Receiving such love helps that person to become open to the abundant love and acceptance that God offers. If you have a bruised and unresponsive spouse, don't give up loving him or her!

Agapē: Decisive Love

In the next chapter, I am going to show how God's love applies pressure on us, pushing us to respond lovingly at all times. Yet although God's love is available for us to use, we don't always want to follow the way of love. When a son walks into his home after school, he shouts: "Mummy! Mummy!" His mother is under some stress because of all she has to do to prepare for some guests who are coming for dinner that day. Her involuntary reaction to the boy's shouting is to snap at him with annoyance: "What?" But God's love within her pushes her in another direction. She responds to the prompting of divine love, controls herself, and calmly says, "What is it, son?" The son excitedly tells the mother, "I have been selected to the school football team!" Hearing this, the mother shouts for joy over her son. What if she had given in to her natural inclination by ignoring the prompting of love? She would have wounded her son deeply and missed an opportunity for family joy.

Obedience is the key that opens the floodgates of God's love. There is no shortage of love in God, as we have said, but we can block its flow by disobedience. Christian love is decisive. It does not always just happen, which is what occurs when we love someone to whom we are attracted. We make it happen through obedience. It is not natural to love our enemies, but we decide to love them. Our decision to obey activates God's love, and we find the strength to do it.

This is the kind of love God has for us. Paul says, "God shows his love for us in that while we were still sinners, Christ died for us" (Rom. 5:8). This brings us to the heart of the Christian understanding of love. It is a decision we make to love even when we do not naturally like to do so and when the object of love does not seem to deserve our love. When the early Christians looked for a word to describe Christian love, they chose the word *agapē* rather than other, commoner words used in those days, such as *philia*. It seems that they wanted to distinguish Christian love from the prevailing understandings of love.

Let's look at some examples of how *agapē* works in the home.

- Paul says that love is not "rude" (1 Cor. 13:5). But often conversation in the home *is* rude. The home seems to be a hard place to practice politeness. We are expected to be polite in our jobs and in church. So we act politely, whether we feel like it or not. But we do not need to playact at home, so children naturally tend to be impolite when talking to their parents, and the parents do the same thing when talking at home. I once read about a pastor's wife who told her husband: "Let's do an exchange today. Why don't you behave at home the way you behave at church and behave at church the way you behave at home?" Most families need a good dose of Paul's advice: "Let your speech always be gracious" (Col. 4:6). Even though we may not naturally like to speak politely and respectfully at home, we can decide to do so as an act of obedience to God. God's love will give us the strength to do that.
- A person is preoccupied with a problem at work. He thinks about it all the time. One day at home, while he is thinking about this problem and attending to a lot of email, he rushes to the kitchen for a glass of water and passes his wife, who is seated at the dining table. Something prompts him to stop and give his wife a hug. To do so is a jarring diversion to his focused mind. Yet he listens to the voice of love and decides to spend a minute or two with his wife.
- A man in an office begins to chat with a married Christian woman, and the conversations turn flirtatious. At first, she enjoys the attention this person is giving her. Then love tells her that this kind of enjoyment is to be had only with her husband, and she refuses her natural tendency to encourage the conversations. Instead, she politely expresses her

disinterest in continuing them. She determines that she will seek this kind of satisfaction only with her husband.

- A husband for whom efficiency and speed are very important values finds himself married to a godly woman who works very slowly. He is often tempted to lash out in impatience. But love makes him decide that the words that come to his mouth must be nipped in the bud. Instead, he focuses on her many good points and "in humility count[s] [her] more significant than [himself]" (Phil. 2:3). He decides to replace disdain for her weaknesses with admiration for her good points.

- I have always had problems with forgetfulness and carelessness. This problem is getting worse as I get older. I waste a lot of time looking for my keys, my glasses, my phone, my notes, and so forth. I often forget to take my phone with me when I leave home. I come home having forgotten to purchase something I promised my wife I would get. This is tough on my wife. She often has to join my searches as I desperately look for something before leaving home. I once told her that, if we wanted to, we could convert our home into a war zone by reacting strongly whenever we get on each other's nerves. But the Bible says, "Love is patient" (1 Cor. 13:4). So we decide not to give expression to the impatience that arises within. There is so much to enjoy in each other that we don't need to get annoyed over our weaknesses.

It is very easy for couples to take each other for granted and, in the process, to overlook expressing their love and concern for each other. H. Norman Wright advises couples, "Make the first four minutes together (morning, evening, and so on) quality time for building and affirming daily affection."[2] While I do not follow this advice exactly, I have found the principle very helpful. We must regularly stop to communicate to our spouses in some way that they are the most important people in our lives. A hug when you see your spouse for the first time in the morning, an inquiry about how he/she slept or how the day went at home or the office, a call in the midst of a busy day to ask how your spouse is doing: these are ways to affirm love.

When I am traveling, I usually send my wife several text or WhatsApp messages a day, just so that she will know what I am doing and that I am thinking about her. Some people say, "I don't need to do things like this because he/she knows that I am thinking about him/her." Even if that is true, stopping frequently to affirm love helps the love to remain fresh and enjoyable. These are aspects of the *agapē* principle of deciding to express love to our spouses.

Before closing this chapter, let me mention one challenging aspect of *agapē* love that can be described as an end in itself rather than the means to an end. It is the call to care for aged parents and family members. Some cannot respond to our love because of their deteriorating mental and physical abilities. Some, such as people suffering from Alzheimer's disease, are very different from the people we knew because their behavior and characteristics have completely changed. Helping them seems to produce no earthly fruit. So we love them without anticipating a positive response from them. We do so because that is what children do with their aged parents. Perhaps it is because Christians were tempted to overlook this duty that Paul uses strong language in his passage about caring for widows. He says, "But if anyone does not provide for his relatives, and especially for members of his household, he has denied the faith and is worse than an unbeliever" (1 Tim. 5:8).

Conclusion

Loving people in the home will continue to be a challenge. There is much that we have to learn here, and we will do so as long as we live. Therefore, we will use the next chapter also to look at some of the details of what it means to love in the home.

4

God's Beautiful Plan

We ended the last chapter by affirming that, as long as we live, we will be learning how to love as Christians in the home. Fortunately, the Bible gives us many guidelines about this. In this chapter, we will look at some of those guidelines.

God's Plan Harmonizes with Human Nature

The Bible's key teaching regarding the roles of husband and wife could be summarized as follows: husbands must sacrificially love their wives, and wives should respectfully submit to their husbands.

Husbands Love Their Wives

Ephesians 5:25 says, "Husbands, love your wives, as Christ loved the church and gave himself up for her." Verse 28 says: "In the same way husbands should love their wives as their own bodies. He who loves his wife loves himself." The first verse suggests that husbands should be willing to die for their wives. When a wife hears that, she might say something like this: "Don't ask my husband to die for me; what I want is something much more simple. Ask him to talk to me when he comes back from work, after I have been struggling alone all day with my naughty children!" Actually, it might be a kind of death for the husband to talk to his wife at that time! If he is stressed out after a heavy day at work, he might not be inclined to engage in a conversation with his wife the moment he comes home. Instead, he might prefer to lie down in bed or watch some TV. Love makes him die to that desire and talk instead.

Colossians introduces the idea of harshness. Paul says, "Husbands, love your wives, and do not be harsh with them" (Col. 3:19). Commenting on this verse, Warren Wiersbe says: "Headship is not dictatorship or lordship. It is loving leadership."[1] The opposite of harshness—honor—is seen in Peter's advice: "Likewise, husbands, live with your wives in an understanding way, showing honor to the woman as the weaker vessel, since they are heirs with you of the grace of life, so that your prayers may not be hindered" (1 Pet. 3:7). Nowhere does the Bible say that husbands should force their wives into submission. Submission is something wives gladly give to husbands who love them and treat them with honor. When selfishness and harshness enter, a relationship becomes abusive. Sadly, this has happened so much that people are revolting against the whole idea that women should be submissive. That is not the answer! The biblical answer is for husbands to love their wives and treat them with honor. Peter tells husbands that if they do this, their "prayers [will] not be hindered." God will not answer the prayers of those who do not love and honor their wives!

Loving with honor is the way for a husband to bring completion to his wife. Women are completed by receiving affection. That is the way they are made. I asked the wives of some of our Youth for Christ staff how they would like their husbands to express their love for them. Here are some of the answers I got. They said, "I want him to:

- believe me."
- speak well of me and not speak of my weaknesses before others, especially before his family."

- point out my errors lovingly without shouting at me."
- speak nicely when he is upset with me."
- appreciate what I do and praise me."
- help with the work around the house, especially looking after the child; words are not enough."
- volunteer to help me with my chores."
- take his weekly day off without fail and do things I like to do on that day."
- be concerned for my spiritual and other welfare."
- inquire how I am faring."
- act quickly when I express a need."
- look after himself, be well groomed and clean."
- listen to me."
- understand me."
- tell me if he is coming late."
- take me out on a date."

I was surprised that none of the wives talked about their husbands buying things for them, especially because I know that all of our staff workers are struggling to make ends meet financially! But every point in this list fits in with the love-and-honor model for husbands advocated in the New Testament. Husbands need to work hard to find what their wives like and try their best to provide them with those things.

Sometimes husbands think that if they provide financially for the family, they have fulfilled their role. Not so! I am sure you have heard the statement, "The best thing a father can do for his children is to love their mother." We husbands must do all we can to tangibly express affection to our wives.

Wives Submit to and Honor Their Husbands

Several times, wives are asked to submit to their husbands (Eph. 5:22, 24; Col. 3:18; 1 Pet. 3:1). Now when there is no love and honoring by the husbands, as taught in the New Testament, this scheme can go horribly wrong. Biblical husbands are humble people who have learned to "submit to Christ, local church leadership and discipline, civil authorities, and their employers."[2] Such a person is qualified to be the head of the home. And when a wife freely submits to loving headship, there is happy, harmonious family life.

Willing submission by the wife is also a way to complete the husband. Paul expands on this in Ephesians 5:33, where he says, "Let the wife see that she respects her husband." The word translated as "respect" can mean "fear," but here the meaning is that of "respecting." Men are completed by receiving respect. To treat a husband disrespectfully is an assault on his personality. Often the wife is the more "righteous" or religious one in the family. But she can be rude and condemnatory in the way she speaks to her husband. That is not the biblical model. Three times the book of Proverbs talks about the terrible experience of living with a nagging wife. Here is one of these: "An endless dripping on a rainy day and a nagging wife are alike" (Prov. 27:15 HCSB; see also 21:9; 25:24). Husbands with such wives might seek ways of escape, such as liquor, affairs, taking on excessive work, or spending too much time with friends.

Peter's advice to wives with unbelieving husbands is relevant to all wives: "Likewise, wives, be subject to your own husbands, so that even if some do not obey the word, they may be won without a word by the conduct of their wives, when they see your respectful and pure conduct" (1 Pet. 3:1–2).

Dr. Emerson Eggerichs has written a helpful book on husband-wife relationships called *Love and Respect.* He says, "The best way to love a husband is to show him respect in ways that are meaningful to him."[3] So the wife needs to take an interest in things that he likes passionately, such as sports, politics, or his intellectual pursuits. While she does not have to become an expert in these areas, out of love for her husband, she makes an effort to get acquainted with them. Loneliness is the lot of anyone who has passionate interests, but that loneliness can be reduced if the spouse is willing to carry on a conversation related to those interests.

We usually tend to automatically do what we have seen our parents do. So if a woman's mother spoke rudely to her husband, the daughter may automatically tend to do the same. She must always be mindful of the fact that this is wrong and make a conscious effort to overcome that habit. Sometimes the husband hits his wife when he is angry. Because that is so common, even Christian men can be tempted to assault their wives when they are upset. That is wicked! Often it is almost a reflex action that is triggered by extreme anger. Husbands need to be forewarned of this terrible danger and be alert to resist the temptation. If a husband does fall, he must immediately do something about it. I recommend that he not only humbly seek forgiveness from his wife, but also share with someone to whom he is accountable. The appearance of this tendency to assault needs firm treatment. It is helpful for someone to come in to hold the man accountable through discipline or some other means. The church also needs to mention this often from the pulpit as something for which Christians have zero tolerance.

A main thesis of Eggerichs's book is that in most cases of marital conflict, the root cause is the failure of the husband to show love to his wife and/or the failure of the wife to show respect to her husband. It would be good for every couple to be alert to this issue. So when there is a conflict, the husband should ask, "Have I failed to love my wife as I should?" and the wife should ask, "Have I failed to respect my husband as I should?"

God's Love Gives Us the Strength

In this and the previous chapter, I have presented biblical models of love that seem admirable. Yet many may wonder whether they are practical. Is it really possible to love in the home the way the Bible asks us to? The first thing I must say in response is that it is God who gives us the strength to love in this way. Paul says, "God's love has been poured into our hearts through the Holy Spirit who has been given to us" (Rom. 5:5). The word translated as "poured" has the idea of abundance. There is no shortage of this love that comes into our lives. Christian leaders who try to be good family members can testify that life is tough; it is emotionally draining and physically exhausting. But there is enough of God's love to give us the strength to keep on loving in spite of the strain. There is enough joy over God's love to us to keep us positive about a life of living for others.

The secret of strength for service (at home, at church, or in society) is God's love in our hearts. Speaking about his life of service, Paul says, "The love of Christ controls us" (2 Cor. 5:14). The word translated as "controls" (*sunechō*) carries the idea of pressing us to action. God's love prompts us to love and gives us the strength to do the sometimes-difficult work of loving.

When my son was a child, he sometimes asked me to play cricket with him in the evening. Often I was tired and preferred to do something else, like reading or watching TV. And, unlike my son, I was not a good cricketer! But love pressed me to go and play. I have never regretted the decision to go, for I always felt physically and emotionally refreshed after playing. Love prompted me to play with my son, and then love refreshed me through the act of playing.

We must be in a position to receive God's love into our lives in order to have the strength to love. First of all, we need to open ourselves to this love. In the first chapter, we spoke of a mother who attributed her nearness to God, despite the strains of bringing up many children, to times she would sit on a chair in prayer with her apron over her head. Isaiah tells us that waiting for God is the secret of strength: "They who wait for the LORD shall renew their strength; they shall mount up with wings like eagles; they shall run and not be weary; they shall walk and not faint" (Isa. 40:31). As we linger in the presence of our loving Father, love floods into our lives. Of course, leaders with families to care for face a challenge in finding time to be alone with God. But as I heard a visiting preacher from America, Lud Golz, say when I was young, "If you are too busy to pray, you are too busy." That piece of advice has never left me!

I am convinced that one of the most important areas of growth in the Christian life is that of learning to accept God's overflowing love for us. It is something we accept in faith, believing what the Bible says about God's love. But some have been so bruised in life that they cannot even accept that they are acceptable to God. The joy of God delighting in them, which the Bible talks about so often (e.g., Pss. 35:27; 147:11; 149:4; Isa. 62:4; Zeph. 3:17), is not real to them. So they live with the pain of the rejection they have experienced on earth. This, in turn, clouds their experience, even their experience of receiving God's love. This makes it difficult for them to joyfully extend love to others.

As we pointed out in the last chapter, some Christians need healing from painful experiences that have left them wounded and unable to enjoy receiving love. Others can guide them to forgive those who have wounded them and to accept the truth that God is going to use the wounding to achieve something good in their lives. Healing in this way can open them to God's love so that they do not look at life from the background of pain and anger over being wounded. The key to this healing is believing what the Bible says about God's relationship with us. Sadly, some refuse to believe this. They want to nurture their anger and hurt about what has been done to them. They hurt themselves and invariably end up hurting others by their actions, which flow from their lack of joy over life.

Some people do not respond to loving concern from family members because they are facing unusual pressures and are in a bad mood as a result. The pressure may be caused by a physical condition, such as a woman's monthly period or menopause; a sickness; an unusual load of work; or special challenges in one's workplace. Take the case of a young mother who has given birth to her second child. Caring for one baby was tough, and caring for two is even more difficult. Her husband goes out of his way to help her, but he is hurt that she does not appreciate his sacrifices. However, she may be responding rudely to him because she is so burdened by her responsibilities that she is constantly in a bad mood. If the husband takes offense at her reactions, it aggravates the problem, causing deeper hurt to his already hurting wife. He has to learn to bear with his wife patiently, do all he can to reduce her pressure, and pray that she will be able to handle the pressure she experiences better.

Sometimes our own sin can block God's love. When there are unconfessed sins in our lives, we tend to act out of the guilt we feel about them. So we become irritable and judgmental. The answer is to "walk in the light," that is, confess our sin, so that "the blood of Jesus . . . cleanses us from all sin" (1 John 1:7). The result of such confession is, as David said after repenting, that "the joy of [God's] salvation" is restored and we "hear joy and gladness" (Ps. 51:12, 8). I know of situations in which everyone in the family knows that the father has done something wrong, but no one confronts him about it. They keep up appearances as if nothing unusual has happened. But there is a heavy mist of unconfessed sin in that home, and the freedom of love is lost.

If you are missing the joy of being freely loved by God and others, do something about it! God has provided ways of healing. If we do not let God heal us, we are going to continue in our unhappiness, and because of that, we will bring unhappiness to our family members also. We cannot afford to cling to our anger and sin. It hurts us and others too much when we do so.

The Balanced Life Is Often Our Cross

Christians are called to a balanced life. That does not mean doing everything in moderation; rather, it means being obedient in every area of life. That is a difficult task in this busy world. Being committed to doing our jobs or studies well while being active in church and also being good family members can be very tiring. We cannot predict some of the needs that will arise in those areas.

One spouse might be upset at night when the other desperately wants to sleep. Disunity might surface right in the middle of a busy program. A child might need help with his studies at a time when a parent prefers to watch television. At each of these times, we need to stretch ourselves and do what has to be done for the sake of our families.

Many people who work hard at their jobs or at Christian service do not give the serious attention to their homes that they should. We often look at these people and put their failings down to sheer commitment to their tasks. Actually, they are due to lack of discipline and disobedience to God's ways. Others who are very committed to caring for their families do not do their jobs or their ministries conscientiously. They are also shirking their responsibilities. Doing all of this can be very taxing at times, but that is something we embrace as part of the cross that goes with being a Christian. I believe that for many Christians, their cross is living the balanced life.

Sometimes emergencies cause us to be stretched. It is Saturday evening, and a pastor's preparation for Sunday's sermon is not complete. However, his daughter has fallen ill. She needs to be taken to the doctor's office. His wife could take the daughter without him. But seeing how much stress she is under, he joins in. When our children get sick, we don't say that attending to them is not in our datebooks! We just do what needs to be done. Yet the sermon for Sunday morning has to be prepared. The pastor cannot slack off there. Losing four hours of preparation time means that he is going to lose four hours of sleep time! But he comes home and does the work that is necessary to have a good sermon ready the next morning.

I must add that one who is active in ministry as a single person cannot keep the same lifestyle once he or she gets married. Incarnational ministry involves lingering with people and making time for long chats. Yet, once a person is married, he or she must do that without sacrificing time for the family. Now the family is also part of his or her ministry. Often, those we minister to do not appreciate that change. We must do our best to help them understand that there is a new normal after marriage.

Sometimes a person fails to recognize this and gives so much time for ministry in the first years of marriage that he neglects his home responsibilities. We'll take the case of a husband in ministry. When his wife complains about his neglect of the home, he tells her that he must follow God's call. The wife, being a devout Christian, chooses not to "fight God" and bears with her husband's neglect of the home. After some years, however, the wife realizes that this neglect was not God's will but the result of her husband's lack of discipline. The consequence may be unpleasant confrontations at home. The guilt-ridden husband, by now suffering from something close to burnout as a result of his poor discipline, goes to the other extreme. He drops out of ministry or takes a job that brings material comfort to the home but takes him away from his call—or keeps his positions in ministry without properly fulfilling his responsibilities.

It is significant that, in ancient Israel, men who were recently married were exempted from war or other civic duties that would have taken them away from their homes. The reason? "For one year he is to be free to stay at home and bring happiness to the wife he has married" (Deut. 24:5 NIV). One of the husband's primary callings is to bring happiness to his wife. That is a good ambition for every husband to have. We must teach couples in volunteer or full-time ministry to practice the balanced life right from the start of their married lives.

Nehemiah was a great leader who achieved amazing results through his costly service on behalf of God's people. He left his comfortable position as the king's cupbearer and went to Jerusalem to lead a challenging and dangerous project. He brilliantly led the people and completed the rebuilding of the wall of Jerusalem, even though he faced huge obstacles. After he received the king's approval for his proposal to rebuild the wall, he asked for "a letter to Asaph, the keeper of the king's forest, that he may give me timber to make beams for the gates of the fortress of the temple, and for the wall of the city, and for the house that I shall occupy" (Neh. 2:8). Notice how he sought timber not only for all his work, but also for the building of his house—probably his ancestral home, which was in a state of disrepair.

Some of God's servants who work very hard on matters related to ministry don't give the necessary time for meeting important family needs—such as keeping the house in good repair or ensuring that the family has a house to live in. A pastor may be so busy that he delays taking his wife to the doctor over an ailment. When he finally goes, they realize that the problem is a serious one, such as cancer, which should have been treated right at the onset. There are many pastors' children who are angry about their fathers' neglect of such matters, which has caused big problems for the families involved. Sometimes these problems surface only later in life. We must not neglect difficult and time-consuming projects relating to the family because we are very busy with ministry responsibilities.

Conclusion

Love has many ramifications when applied to life in the home. We learn more and more of the richness of love as we proceed through the years of marriage. If we have made loving our family members our aim in life, our lives will be an unending journey of exploration into the beauty of family life. We cannot overestimate the legacy of multiple acts of sacrificial kindness and consideration within the family. There is amazing joy and security in knowing that family members truly love each other and want the best for each other.

5

Sexual Love

When we speak about love in today's sex-saturated culture, people immediately think about sex. Sadly, however, when many people think about enjoying sex, they do not think about relations between husband and wife. Philip Ryken quotes some research that shows that "with all the encounters and innuendoes, the average American views sexual material more than ten thousand times a year."[1] He says that "by a ratio of more than ten to one, the couplings on television involve sex outside marriage."[2] A TV producer, explaining why sexual situations on TV are generally between unmarried couples, said, "Married or celibate characters aren't as much fun."[3] A famous Indian actress, when interviewed by *The Times of India*, said: "Monogamy is weird. One is boring."[4]

Our response to such attitudes must not be to underestimate the value of sex in marriage, but to look for biblical guidelines about sex. The Bible gives an important place to sex and sees it as a major expression of love between husband and wife.

Why God Created Sex

While I do not intend to go into a major discussion of sex in marriage in this book, it would be good to summarize the reasons given for sex in the Bible. Five reasons can be listed.

The most obvious reason is *childbearing*. The first command given to humans by the Creator was, "Be fruitful and multiply and fill the earth" (Gen. 1:28). In our discussion of children in chapter 10, we will show how important this responsibility is and how the devotion to convenience today has resulted in many coming to see the upbringing of children as a nuisance.

The second reason for sex is that it is *a key aspect of the unity between husband and wife*. When God instituted marriage, he said, "Therefore a man shall leave his father and his mother and hold fast to his wife, and they shall become one flesh" (Gen. 2:24). This statement that two become one flesh is an affirmation of sexual unity in marriage and is repeated six times in the New Testament (Matt. 19:5–6; Mark 10:7–8; 1 Cor. 6:16; Eph. 5:31). This underscores how important sexual unity is to a marriage. If a sexual relationship is a means to unity, it is not something to be done in a hurry. A couple cannot be truly one physically if they are not one in mind and spirit. So lingering conversation is a key prelude to the sexual relationship; time needs to be given to talk to get caught up on each other's lives. The order is first mental and spiritual oneness, followed by physical oneness. In fact, sex becomes an incentive to unity. Knowing that they cannot really enjoy sex without being united, a couple is challenged to strive for unity, spurred by the prospect of sexual relations.

The third reason for sex is *giving to and receiving from each other*. The discussions on sex in Proverbs and Song of Solomon shows that love is given and received during sex. The couple learns how to bring happiness to each other. Each is sensitive to what the other likes and dislikes. They talk about this and find out how they can give love to each other. Sex is most pleasurable when one enjoys and also brings enjoyment to the other. Love is not a solitary act. It is completed when there is mutual sharing of enjoyment of each other and with each other.

The fourth reason for sex is *receiving sensual, physical pleasure*. Shyness over this has caused some to look at the book of

Song of Solomon primarily as an allegory describing a human's relationship with God. While one could read the book in this way, it is not the primary purpose of the book. In his beautiful book *Sex, Romance, and the Glory of God*, C. J. Mahaney describes Song of Solomon as "an eight-chapter feast of unbridled, uninhibited, joyous immersion in verbal and physical expressions of passion between a man and a woman."[5] This theme must be very important if the Holy Spirit inspired such a large book on it and included it in the canon of Scripture. Christians must learn to look at sex as a holy, spiritual, and physical act that pleases God.

While many Christians consider such talk inappropriate, especially for women, we can and should affirm that sexual desire is good. Of course, single people must learn to control this desire. Married couples embark on a journey of learning to satisfy each other's desire and to find satisfaction exclusively with each other.

Maintaining a biblical perspective on sexual love is a challenge today. The culture presents an idea of sexual enjoyment that is unattainable by most couples. The media define *sexy* according to physical characteristics of which most people fall short. So we have annual selections for the sexiest man and sexiest woman in the world. Most of our spouses won't make it to those lists. But Christianity teaches that the fullest enjoyment of sex is between people who are committed to each other for life. That commitment gives them the freedom to give themselves fully to their physical enjoyment. The common cultural practice is for people to make themselves look beautiful when they go outside the home. Therefore, many may not be particularly concerned about what they look like at home. The teaching of Song of Solomon and Proverbs is that a major reason to look beautiful is to please one's spouse.

I remember reading an article on how difficult it is for supermodels to have happy marriages. It said that they concentrate so much on acting sexy before others that it is difficult for them to behave in a genuinely loving way with their spouses. The deepest fulfillments in Christianity are through relationships of commitment. Christians must discipline themselves to keep their sexual enjoyment within their marriages.

Many years ago, on a flight back home, I saw a film starring Jennifer Lopez. I told my then teenage son, "Jennifer Lopez is very beautiful." He laughed and said, "Millions of men all over the world will agree with you on that!" Then I told him, "But when I get up in the morning, there is no one I'd rather see than your mother." Yes, there are some extraordinarily beautiful people on earth. But we learn to find the greatest beauty in our spouses. I think every married Christian must ask himself or herself, "Have I communicated to my spouse the idea that I see him/her as a truly beautiful person?" If our spouses do not see us as looking at them as beautiful, it's we who have failed, not they.

Song of Solomon shows that men and women meditate on physical aspects of their spouses and express the fruit of their meditation in words. Consider the following meditation by the husband:

> How beautiful and pleasant you are, O loved one, with all your delights! Your stature is like a palm tree, and your breasts are like its clusters. I say I will climb the palm tree and lay hold of its fruit. Oh may your breasts be like clusters of the vine, and the scent of your breath like apples, and your mouth like the best wine. (Song 7:6–9)

And here is a meditation by the wife:

> My beloved is radiant and ruddy, distinguished among ten thousand. His head is the finest gold; his locks are wavy, black as a raven. His eyes are like doves beside streams of water, bathed in milk, sitting beside a full pool. His cheeks are like beds of spices, mounds of sweet-smelling herbs. His lips are lilies, dripping liquid myrrh. His arms are rods of gold, set with jewels. His body is polished ivory, bedecked with sapphires. His legs are alabaster columns, set on bases of gold. His appearance is like Lebanon, choice as the cedars. His mouth is

most sweet, and he is altogether desirable. This is my beloved and this is my friend, O daughters of Jerusalem. (Song 5:10–16)

The above, of course, implies that we must keep ourselves well-groomed for our spouses. The earlier passage speaks of "the scent of your breath like apples, and your mouth like the best wine." If this is to be true, our teeth must be well brushed! Cleanliness is a key feature of sexual relations!

The fifth reason for sex is that *it mirrors our relationship with Christ*. After stating that "the two shall become one flesh" (Eph. 5:31) in marriage, Paul says, "This mystery is profound, and I am saying that it refers to Christ and the church" (v. 32). When Paul uses the term *mystery*, he is talking about something hidden that has now been revealed in the gospel. He is saying that there is something amazing about the depth of oneness we share with Christ. An illustration of this is the physical union between man and wife. There are many similar features in these two kinds of relationship. Both include openness, total devotion, give and take, understanding, communication, and ecstatic love. It is not an accident that in the Old Testament, the word *know* is used both for knowing God (1 Sam. 3:7; Jer. 31:34) and for sexual relationships (e.g., Gen. 4:1, 17). Biblically, one way people can begin to understand the relationship between God (and Christ) and Christians is by looking at a good husband-and-wife relationship.

Sexual Love Gives Security to the Marriage Relationship

First Corinthians 7 discusses numerous issues relating to marriage. The first seven verses deal with the issue of couples maintaining sexual relations. Verse 3 says, "The husband should fulfill his wife's sexual needs, and the wife should fulfill her husband's needs" (NLT). Paul addresses those wanting to abstain from sexual relations in order to spend more time in prayer, saying, "Do not deprive one another, except perhaps by agreement for a limited time, that you may devote yourselves to prayer" (v. 5a). But as Paul says, this is to be only for a limited time. He goes on to say, "but then come together again, so that Satan may not tempt you because of your lack of self-control" (v. 5b). The implication is that couples who are not having regular sexual relations may be making themselves unnecessarily vulnerable to the temptation to commit adultery.

I suppose that few people today abstain from sexual relations because they want to be separated for prayer. A far more common reason for not having relations is busyness and tiredness. This problem is difficult to solve in our fast-paced world. Some resort to pornography as an alternative. This is less demanding in terms of emotional involvement, but destructive in terms of marital happiness. Busy people must conscientiously give priority to sexual relations in their marital life. We somehow make the time for the things that we consider essential.

Using some fairly explicit language, Proverbs 5:15–20 argues that one way for a man to avoid adultery is to find sexual satisfaction with "the wife of his youth":

> Drink water from your own cistern,
>> flowing water from your own well.
> Should your springs be scattered abroad,
>> streams of water in the streets?
> Let them be for yourself alone,
>> and not for strangers with you.
> Let your fountain be blessed,
>> and rejoice in the wife of your youth,
> a lovely deer, a graceful doe.
> Let her breasts fill you at all times with delight;
>> be intoxicated always in her love.
> Why should you be intoxicated, my son,
>> with a forbidden woman
> and embrace the bosom of an adulteress?

This is one reason why I do not advocate couples having long separations from each other, such as happens when one spouse goes to another country or region for work. Those of us who travel a lot should be careful not to have long separations from our families.

There is an idea among some Christians, even very committed Christians, that once you have two or three children, the time of having sexual relations is past. I know of homes where the wife has moved out of the couple's bedroom after about ten to fifteen years of marriage and sleeps with the children. She refuses to have sexual relations with her husband. This is a violation of God's plan for marriage—as such, we could call this an unholy or ungodly relationship.

In the passage from Proverbs quoted above, an older man is exhorted to sexually enjoy the body of "the wife of your youth" (5:18). The statement "Let her breasts fill you at all times with delight; be intoxicated always in her love" (v. 19) shows, as Bruce Waltke points out, that "the quality of her lovemaking is totally satisfying."[6] Every couple should have this as a goal in their relationship. According to Proverbs, a side effect of such enjoyment is security against an illicit relationship.

Four times the Bible describes the marriage tie as the husband holding fast (or cleaving) to his wife (Gen. 2:24; Matt. 19:5; Mark 10:7; Eph. 5:31). The Greek word translated as "hold fast"[7] means "to cling, to glue, to cement." In all these references, after saying, "hold fast to his wife," the passages go on to say, "and the two shall become one flesh." As Leon Morris puts it, "This refers to the sexual act, which unites husband and wife in the most intimate fashion."[8] Sexual unity is a key ingredient of the glue or cement that binds a couple together.

There was a time when lust was considered primarily a problem with which men struggled. That has been shown to be wrong—it is an issue for women also.[9] In our ministry, several young men have talked about being sexually used by older women. Yet it is true that wives often do not understand how important sexual relations are to a man. Willard F. Harley Jr., in his influential book *His Needs, Her Needs: Building an Affair Proof Marriage*, says, "The typical wife doesn't understand her husband's deep need for sex any more than the typical husband understands his wife's deep need for affection."[10] When a wife refuses her husband's request for sex, it is a big blow to him. Someone has compared it to being slapped by his wife. But that does not give the husband permission to slap his wife in return. After all, Christians are those who turn the other check when slapped (Matt. 5:39). Husbands must be sensitive to their wives' moods and never force themselves on them. Yet, when a husband's request for sex is rejected, he can come under severe temptation. Husbands need to be much in prayer to overcome this.

Often the husband does not think of or romance his wife at all during the day, then suddenly asks for sex at night. But that kind of behavior is not good preparation for sexual intercourse, especially for the woman. Though husbands may be able to be turned on in this way, women are fulfilled through affection. H. Norman Wright says: "Some women have complained that the only time their husbands expressed affection to them was when they wanted intercourse. Affection and attention should occur every day whether intercourse is intended or not."[11]

Problematic Sexual Experiences and Attitudes

Yet the issue is not so simple. To many women, sex is unpleasant. My wife has told me that some ladies she knows describe sexual intercourse with words such as "when my husband wants to trouble me . . ." They see it as a nuisance that does not give them any satisfaction. A Christian woman once said, referring to sexual intercourse, "My husband treats me as his trash can." However, the Bible presents sexual relations as something that both husband and wife enjoy.

Many Christians do not go into marriage with a biblical attitude toward sex. How important it is to communicate this to our youth. Often they get their first information about sex from non-Christian sources, so the ideas they get often contradict what the Bible says. It is especially important for us to communicate to our children the truth that the most fulfilling kind of sexual relationship is between two people who are committed to each other in love for life. Research shows that married couples, especially those married for many years, generally enjoy sexual relations more than cohabiting couples.[12] Today, however, the world considers sex outside marriage almost as a normal practice. That is the message young people get from the culture they live in—and their hormones agree! With our youth facing such a serious challenge from the world, the church will seriously fail them if it does not give clear and consistent teaching on this issue. An extended comment from Daniel Heimbach is worth repeating:

> The positive principles at stake seem to be that sex outside of marriage erodes and ultimately destroys the precious value of exclusivity and selflessness in the sexual relationship. . . . Adulterous sex can never be exclusive and selfless. By its very nature, adulterous sex rejects the value of keeping sex exclusive and is driven by self-centered interests that preempt our responsibility to always do what is best for others—in this case those depending on us in the areas of marriage and family life. But the value of exclusive, selfless sex is so good that God never allows less. *He prohibits sex outside of marriage to keep us from losing what is best.*[13]

For those who started their marriages on the wrong footing sexually, let me say that it is not too late to change that. As we have implied above, many do not have happy sexual relationships with their spouses because of premarital sexual experiences, like that of being sexually abused. There is healing for such wounds through the grace of God mediated through a skillful counselor, pastor, leader, or friend. People who were sexually promiscuous before marriage may need special assurance of the purity that comes by the forgiveness they receive through the blood of Christ before they can start having healthy relations with their spouses. Couples should look for people they can trust who will help them in this area. I know of several couples who, though they outwardly seem happy, did not have proper sexual relationships for some years. When they finally plucked up the courage to talk to someone about it, they realized that the problem was solvable.

Yet there are some who may never have good sexual experiences, even with the help of skillful counselors. I refer to people whose spouses have physical problems or illnesses that make sexual relations difficult or impossible. Some may never fully recover from wounds of the past, such as rape. We can also include here couples who are geographically separated for a considerable time. This is not easy in our sex-saturated culture, where sexual satisfaction is viewed as a human right and therefore necessary for an authentic life. Despite what people say, research has demonstrated that sex is not a biological necessity. Abstinence from sexual relations does not harm people. Therefore, in Christianity, abstinence is a high value.

A common solution today's married people find for the inability to have sexual relations is masturbation, which they view as a harmless means of releasing sexual tension. They argue that the Bible does not prohibit this. While that may be true, it is also true that masturbation is usually preceded by lustful thoughts, which are clearly condemned in Scripture. Sometimes the prospect of this pleasure leads one to expose oneself to unclean material, such as pornography. Also, it invariably leads people to find sources of pleasure outside of their spouses, and this harms them and their marriages. For these reasons, masturbation should not be viewed as a legitimate means of releasing sexual pressure.

A key to victory here is refusing to succumb to the cultural message that everyone has a right to sexual gratification. If we accept this, we can begin to look to some form of gratification as an indispensable part of a complete life. This attitude must be battled, as it is damaging to our well-being.

Masturbation is not the end of the world for the Christian. If one succumbs to it, he or she must immediately go to God in confession, naming the particular sins that led to it, and receive his forgiveness and cleansing (1 John 1:9).

Christians abstain from sexual relationships until they get married. In Christianity, there is a noble line of heroes who were single and remained sexually celibate. At the top of this list is Jesus himself—the most complete and joyous person who ever lived. There are devout Christians with homosexual desires who have chosen the path of celibacy. Some are able to change and become heterosexual. Others may have to struggle with homosexual desire while remaining celibate until death.

Because sexual desire is such a strong force, I do not recommend long engagements. In a sex-saturated world, when one is in close contact with the person one intends to marry, it is very difficult to abstain from sexual relations over a long engagement. Usually couples delay marriage for economic reasons. Perhaps we should seriously question this thinking. Paul's advice to young widows is appropriate here: "But if they cannot exercise self-control, they should marry. For it is better to marry than to burn with passion" (1 Cor. 7:9).

Given the strong temptation, especially for couples in love, to have sexual relations outside marriage today, it is vitally important for parents and the church to talk often about the sinfulness and dangers of extramarital sex. To fail to do this is to fail our people. This need is all the more urgent today because the culture is bombarding our people with the opposite message very attractively. I fear that because premarital sex has become so popular, Christians are reluctant to offend people by speaking about it. By remaining silent, we may avoid offending some people, but we offend God by failing to present his truth to God's people.

Theologically, we see the challenge of celibacy for people with sexual desires as an aspect of the frustration that Paul says all Christians will face until they see death (see Rom. 8:18–25). These frustrations make them groan as they wait for the redemption of their bodies, which will surely come and will be eternal in duration

(v. 23). We all have areas in life that we find frustrating and that cause us to groan with holy longing for our final redemption. We can groan, but we must not sin. Many today think that what the Bible calls sin, that is, sex outside marriage, is necessary for a full life. But we believe that those without meaningful sexual relationships can also experience the full life that Jesus said he came to give us (John 10:10). Sexual relations are not a basic human right.

This is why we have no sympathy for Christians who have intimate relationships with people outside of marriage and then say as an excuse, "My spouse does not satisfy me." Even such people can have a full life in Christ. How sad I was when I read in the papers that hospital authorities allowed a teenage boy with terminal cancer to have a sexual encounter with a prostitute before he died. That came about from the myth that sexual relations are a human right that must be available to all. The push for ordaining practicing homosexuals to the ministry and the push for homosexual marriage also come from this wrong idea. We say that people with such desires can have fulfilled lives as celibates. We do so with humility, realizing that they have a huge battle ahead of them in our sex-saturated culture. But we believe that the grace of God can help them to live happy and holy lives.

Love Battles Insecurity[14]

Ultimately, every wrong sexual affair is an expression of insecurity. The ego gratification that comes from the attention and adoration of another person or from the sense of conquest—of having "won" over someone—causes one to be blind to all the negatives that come with an affair. Most people are lured into wrong relationships not so much by sex as by the sense of self-affirmation that comes from the affairs. Sometimes we hear people say, "With such a beautiful wife, why did he start an affair with a person who is not half as attractive?" Invariably that man was not attracted by the woman's physical beauty. The attention that she paid him, or that he was able to pay her, served as an ego boost that addressed his sense of insecurity. Sometimes it is the sense of conquering another person's mind and body or of being able to control another person that brings the satisfaction that triggers an affair. The extreme form of such "conquest" is rape.

Dr. Jay Kesler says, "People are most vulnerable to sexual temptation, I've found, when they're unable to achieve their goals, when they're frustrated or they're discouraged, when their dreams are being dashed."[15] This is why people often begin affairs at times when they are having serious problems in their vocations and their vocational value is under question. People's sense of significance, especially that of men, is closely tied to how valued they feel in their vocational life. The sense of self-worth given to a man by an adoring female or by conquering the body of a woman temporarily fills the void of insecurity that he feels about himself.

This insecurity theory explains why many strong political leaders (whose so-called strength could actually be a compensation for insecurity) have multiple affairs with younger people. All the acclaim that leadership brings does not take away their hunger for affirmation and significance. Sadly, the same principle applies to strong Christian leaders who get entangled in affairs. I was so sad to read an article in one of our Sri Lankan newspapers some years ago explaining how, because of their insecurities, politicians and pastors get into affairs despite their power over people. Insecurity has been given as a trigger for affairs that people have in midlife. As Kesler says: "Middle age often brings with it a particular vulnerability to sexual temptation. . . . Some people become frightened about growing older, and they wonder if women still find them attractive. So they're tempted to test the waters to find out."[16]

Busy people, such as medical doctors and those who are involved in ministry, also become vulnerable to affairs if their spouses are not happy about their busyness. They come home to a hostile reception after work. Their spouses keep blaming them for neglecting the family. But at work, they are treated like gods because people admire them for their skill and success. It is easy for people to get ensnared into affairs with colleagues at work who are always affirming them while their spouses are always putting them down.

This same thing is happening now through social media, such as Facebook. People start chatting online in that somewhat artificial world and say things to others that they should be saying only to their spouses. One says to another: "What a comfort you are to me. I was so lonely, and chatting with you has been such a blessing." A person can begin to grow emotionally attracted to such affirmation and be tempted to go deeper and deeper into the relationship. The end result is an affair.

All of these situations are examples of love without responsibility. God made us for committed relationships. Ultimately, affairs end up ruining our lives and the lives of those we love, leaving all affected parties with deep wounds. One cannot hurt one's spouse without hurting oneself. The ties are so deep and so entangled with who we are that we cannot just drop our spouses and replace them with other people. Committed relationships are maintained through hard work. Love without responsibility is easy at first, because it has built an unreal world to define it. But the hurt caused by affairs is great. So we must work hard at our relationships at home. When we keep affirming each other, our vulnerability to affairs is greatly reduced.

An aspect of the hard work that goes into responsible love is staying clear of situations that could lead to unhealthy relationships. Paul's advice to Timothy to "flee youthful passions" (2 Tim. 2:22) applies to adults also. As we said in chapter 2, it is quite natural to like being with certain people of the opposite sex. We naturally find some people more attractive than others. That is not a sin. But we need to be careful in our relationships with these people.

Suppose you are attracted to a colleague at work or in ministry. You enjoy working together, you seem to understand each other, and you do some good work or ministry as a result. But an unhealthy emotional tie can develop, a tie you may not recognize because the relationship started so well and was so pure. Others may alert you to what is happening because they see what you do not. They see what happens when your eyes meet or how you are automatically drawn to each other in a crowded room. When your friends alert you to such dangers, instead of being angry about their "prying into your life," you should be grateful for their advice and practice maximum caution. There have been a few times when I saw what seemed to be signs of indiscreet relationships, but I did not have the confidence to alert the persons involved. How much I regret that, because my fears were confirmed and good people ended up getting badly hurt.

Because you click so well, you may tend to move closer to that person and to talk when you see him or her. We must be careful about too much contact of this kind. Some people insist on helping people of the other sex even though an unhealthy emotional tie has been developing. "I am the only one who understands him/her" can be a dangerous statement when said about a member of the opposite sex. To guard against this, I generally ask my wife to handle a lot of the communication about personal things in the lives of my women colleagues. I also do so out of the conviction that she, as a woman, can do a better job than me with those issues.

Genuine love requires hard work, as we showed in the last chapter, but it is worth it. There is something wonderfully affirming in a relationship that has been forged through the hard work of applying *agapē* love in the home and the hard work of discreet behavior outside the home. The affirmation of family members is a great medicine for insecurity. After all, all of us have insecurities to a greater or lesser extent. Affirming spouses, parents, and children can be great agents of God's grace in combatting these insecurities. These are the most important people in our lives. What better place is there to be affirmed than the home?

But the ultimate cure for insecurity is the thrill of being children of God who are significant because God has a wonderful plan for us. This is why spending unhurried time with God daily is so important. In a passage that warns about the dangers of worldliness and impure thinking, James exhorts: "Draw near to God, and he will draw near to you. Cleanse your hands, you sinners, and purify your hearts, you double-minded" (James 4:8). In our times with God, not only are we fed with God's truth, which gives us a sense of the terribleness of sin, we are also fed with doses of loving affirmation from God, which help to reduce the attractiveness of affairs.

Shame about ourselves is one of the ways insecurity expresses itself. God's affirmation as we spend time with him can take that shame away. David said, "Those who look to him are radiant, and their faces shall never be ashamed" (Ps. 34:5). We look to the eternal God. When we spend time with him, we experience something of the thrill of knowing that the eternal, almighty God considers us his children (1 John 3:1). The Bible says that God delights in us (Pss. 147:11; 149:4). One of the greatest thrills in life is the knowledge that the almighty God looks at us with a smile and exclaims, "He belongs to me" or "She is my precious child." If so, the greatest terror for Christians should be forfeiting the smile of God. This is a great preventative to sexual sin.

Conclusion

However busy and stressed out we may be with our challenges and duties, let us never neglect the thrill of relishing the presence of God. Let us never allow the security of being loved by God to leave us. We are spurred in life by the truth of Deuteronomy 33:27: "The eternal God is your dwelling place, and underneath are the everlasting arms." With such security, whether you are married, single, widowed, or divorced, you can be a happy and fulfilled individual.

6

Joy

It is from the Old Testament that Christians get many of the values that characterize the lifestyle of the people of God. From it we learn something of God's heart and the character he wishes his people to have.

Joy is presented in the Old Testament as one of the key values of a godly lifestyle. There are thirteen Hebrew root words with the idea of joy, and they yield twenty-seven separate words for joy! Two verses in Zephaniah alone (3:14, 17) have a total of eight words for joy.[1] This emphasis is found in the New Testament too. Paul asks Christians to rejoice in the Lord always (Phil. 4:4), and Jesus says that our joy will be full when he gives us his joy (John 15:11). We can safely say that joy affects the health of a home, or, as Proverbs 17:22 puts it, "A joyful [or "cheerful," NIV] heart is good medicine."

It is not surprising, then, that the home is presented in the Old Testament as a happy place. Families are told to be joyful when they worship God and eat together in God's sanctuary (Deut. 12:7, 12; 14:26). Family joy is particularly evident during festivals (Deut. 16:11, 14; 2 Chron. 30:21). The family is asked to be "altogether joyful" as they have their festival meal (Deut. 16:15).

Ecclesiastes advises men, "Enjoy life with the wife whom you love" (Eccl. 9:9). Proverbs tells older men, "Rejoice in the wife of your youth" (Prov. 5:18). The person who has many children is described as "blessed" or "happy" (Ps. 127:5).[2] Families are urged to rejoice in the good that God has done for them (Deut. 26:11).

Joy: The Wealth of a Home

When Sri Lanka endured a violent revolution in 1988–89, life was very troublesome and somewhat dangerous. The schools were closed for months at a time. Many left the country, saying they were going away for the sake of their children. I had just returned from a six-month sabbatical at Gordon-Conwell Theological Seminary in the United States. I had been very happy there, doing things I love to do—such as studying, writing, and teaching. In the middle of the troubles, in 1989, Gordon-Conwell wrote to offer me what looked like a dream job in terms of what I like to do. But my wife and I were convinced that our calling was for lifetime ministry in Sri Lanka, so I declined the invitation. Yet we needed to make it worthwhile for our children that we stayed in Sri Lanka. After all, it was us and not them who had responded to a call to Sri Lanka. When my wife and I talked about this, we decided that the best blessing we could leave to our children was a happy home. Whatever they experienced outside, they should know that they would be coming to a warm, accepting, and happy place.

I soon came to realize that happiness is the real wealth of a home. A husband told his wife, "One day we will be rich, and then we can buy a lot of things." The wife replied: "We are already rich! Maybe we will have a lot of money someday and be able to buy many things." In a discussion on wealth, Paul says, "Godliness with contentment is great gain" (1 Tim. 6:6). He goes on to remind us to think of eternity when choosing our values: "We brought nothing into the world, and we cannot take anything out of the world" (v. 7). Then he says that if we have the essentials

80

of life, we should be satisfied: "But if we have food and clothing, with these we will be content" (v. 8). Finally, he talks of the dangers of desiring to be rich: "But those who desire to be rich fall into temptation, into a snare, into many senseless and harmful desires that plunge people into ruin and destruction" (v. 9). It is easy for Christians to get sucked into a dangerous pursuit of wealth that can ruin their lives and rob them of the precious wealth of contentment. I have seen this happen many times.

Contentment is a characteristic that we need to develop by learning. Paul says: "*I have learned* in whatever situation I am to be content. I know how to be brought low, and I know how to abound. In any and every circumstance, *I have learned* the secret of facing plenty and hunger, abundance and need" (Phil. 4:11b–12). The best place to learn this is the home. We must all strive to have happy and contented homes. Then, even if we don't have much money (and full-time Christian workers in most countries don't), our family members can still think of themselves as wealthy people.

Yet joy, especially joy in the family, is a value with which some people are not familiar. Tim Stafford says: "Most joyful people were raised in a home where they saw joy modeled daily. Joy is a part of their inherited family culture, which they choose to carry on."[3] But many Christians today have not experienced joy as part of their family culture. Joy, then, is a value that has to be learned and consciously practiced. After all, the Bible commands us to be joyful. Therefore, we will look at some practical ways of enhancing joy in the home in this chapter. Chapter 11 will describe why children need to have fun and how we should develop joyful traditions in the home for our children.

Appearance: The Enemy of Joy

As many couples do not pursue joy in the family as an ambition, they are vulnerable to falling into another trap that can end up ruining that joy. This is the trap of slavery to appearance. They think that if they can't be happy, they at least must try to appear successful, rich, or influential. In the pursuit of such goals, they can follow dangerous paths.

The commonest path is spending money that they do not have. They purchase a house they cannot afford. Or they buy things that will make the house look beautiful, even though they do not have sufficient funds to purchase them at that time. When there is a wedding in the family, they spend money they do not have for the reception. The result is that they end up hopelessly in debt to moneylenders, banks, or pawnbrokers. When they are unable to keep up the payments, they lose their spiritual freedom and peace. Also, they are forced to reduce their giving for God's work, and they struggle to pay for essentials such as food, health, and education.

I am amazed at how many people purchase things on credit without seriously calculating how they are going to pay up. In more affluent cultures, this is done by having several credit cards. Funds are taken from one card to pay what is due to another card account. I have seen people who, under heavy pressure to purchase something or to spend on something, take loans after devising impractical payback schemes. They haven't taken into account the possibility of a family member falling ill or some other emergency that they could face. If that happens, they are stuck. They pawn valuable things such as jewelry and often end up having to forfeit them permanently. But more importantly, they remain under bondage to these loans.

In Sri Lanka, people often overspend when they have a family wedding. There is usually a meal or a reception with finger food. Rich wedding cake is considered an essential part of a wedding celebration. Inviting a lot of people and having an expensive reception is often regarded as a sign of status. As a result, many couples start their married life in debt, and their parents are in debt with them. I am amazed at how people overspend even after we leaders have warned them about the dangers of this. Some seem to be caught up in the events so much that they don't realize that they are overspending.

A few years back, I went with several Youth for Christ staff members to the north of Sri Lanka for a wedding of one of our workers. After the wedding service, we had a nice meal and then left for our long journey back home. While we were traveling, one colleague suddenly said: "Hey! They didn't serve us wedding cake." As noted above, wedding cake is regarded as a staple in wedding celebrations in Sri Lanka. In jest, one of those in the van called the bridegroom and asked him, "What happened to the cake?" He said: "When we drew up the budget for the wedding, we realized that we could not afford to have both a meal and the rich wedding cake. So we decided not to have the cake." I told my colleagues, "He's my hero!" He was willing to do without something considered essential so that he could give the guests a good meal without going into debt.

While on the topic of weddings, I need to say that often in Sri Lanka, Christian parents arrange marriages for their children to people living abroad in Western countries. They have the idea that with such marriages, their children could also move to the West and secure a good financial future for the whole family. They base their choices on recommendations of other Christians. But especially in the individualistic Western culture, people can have lifestyles that no one else really knows about. How many disastrous marriages have resulted from this practice, producing deeply regretful parents!

As noted earlier, whether they live in the West or the East, parents must be careful about using appearance as a criterion for encouraging or discouraging a marriage. I have seen parents object to the marriage plans of a Christian who wants to marry another wonderful Christian because they think the potential spouse is socially inferior or not beautiful or handsome enough for their child. They use the color of the person's skin or his or her financial standing as a disqualification. Both the man and the woman love Christ, and there are bright prospects of them living a very happy life together. But for reasons that could be classed under "appearance," the parents object to the marriage. These parents may be Christian leaders or even pastors, but their attitudes are sinful and worldly!

Bondage to appearance is often especially a problem for those who were once poor but have been liberated from poverty. Many Christians I work with grew up in homes ravaged by deprivation because of poverty and alcoholism. Then they came to Christ. They started a journey of discovery of their new identity in Christ. They came to realize that they did not need to feel inferior to people they once considered as being in a higher class. But they still had the scars of the wounds inflicted on them during their upbringing in poor homes. Memories of being laughed at because they wore old shoes and darned clothes to school still remained fresh in their minds. They did not want their children to have such experiences. Now they have wealthy Christian friends as their equals in the church. They feel they have a right to enjoy what those friends have. Advertisements on television entice them with attractive long-term payment options to purchase things they once considered unattainable luxuries. This has been called "the revolution of rising expectations." Those who experience it can end up deeply in debt.

We must remember that equality is not the same as having a lifestyle equal to that of another Christian family. We must live according to our means and be happy with what we have. For example, in Sri Lanka, there are different kinds of schools. The most expensive fees are charged by the so-called international schools. Many Christians have put their children into those schools. There is nothing wrong with that. But some Christians who cannot afford it have also put their children into those schools. They struggle to pay the fees and sometimes get into real trouble because they are unable to do so. Some are forced to pull the children out of school because they have not paid the fees.

When Jesus wanted to teach about the need for us to plan our projects before launching into them, one of the examples he used was that of a building project: "Which of you, desiring to build a tower, does not first sit down and count the cost, whether he has enough to complete it? Otherwise, when he has laid a foundation and is not able to finish, all who see it begin to mock him, saying, 'This man began to build and was not able to finish'" (Luke 14:28–30). We must not allow the desire to acquire or build something that looks nice to cause us to make the foolish decision to overspend.

Some of God's children move away from their call from God in order to achieve financial success. For financial reasons, people called to the ministry may leave the ministry or leave the particular ministry in which they serve to go to a better-paying job in ministry. Some leave their spouses and children and go abroad to work and earn, seeing them only once in two years.

A leader in one of our major denominations in Sri Lanka told me about a common scenario in the lives of many pastors. A pastor's family is not experiencing joy in their home. The family has to sacrifice because of the pastor's ministry. Often he tells them that the sacrifices are because of the call of God. He married the most committed girl in the youth fellowship, and because of her commitment to Christ, she bears up with the deprivation that comes as a result of her pastor husband's neglect. But after about fifteen years of putting up with this, she decides that she has had enough. She realizes that some of the hardship they have endured is because of the pastor's indiscipline or lack of concern rather than because of his obedience to God. She begins to rebel against the husband's call. She makes demands that he cannot fulfill. Not having joy, she at least wants some material things to satisfy her. He cannot meet her demands while being in the ministry. So he makes a vocational change—moving away from his call to a more financially rewarding job.

This scenario can be avoided if the pastor is committed to the joy of his family. There are a lot of joy-producing things that can be done without spending much money. By doing these things, we teach our children that the most valuable experiences in life do not have to be linked with financial resources.

My writer friend Tim Stafford's father was a pastor, and he grew up in a home that could be considered relatively poor. He says: "As a child . . . I felt our lack of status. But remarkably enough, I never felt that we were truly poor." He says that "the key . . . was my parents' aggressive posture. Instead of talking about their lack, they focused on what they had. They tried to help their kids believe they were enjoying the finest things in life: books, music, camping, baseball games." As a result, he says, "we thought we were better off than people who had to buy big cars and steaks to enjoy life." The family's practice of giving also helped buttress this idea that they were a privileged family. Stafford says: "An early vivid memory of mine is my mother late one night writing out checks to various Christian organizations. 'Tithing makes me feel rich,' she said to me as she looked up. 'We have all this money to give away.'"[4]

We are talking about homes that are freed from the deceptive bondage to material prosperity and other means of appearing successful; homes devoted to nurturing children who are contented and happy in the Lord and in the love and commitment of their parents.

Joy Is Extended through Praise

Praise is an important feature of the Christian life. I would go so far as to call it an essential Christian discipline. First and foremost, we praise God. And this praise has many benefits. First, it honors God. Second, it helps us remember truths about God that can get clouded out because of the pressures of life. Third, it helps us enjoy God more. Joy is not complete until it is shared. A gift is not fully enjoyed until we acknowledge our appreciation of it to the donor. So praise is one of the pathways to joy in the Christian life.

Just as we praise God, we also praise people because we enjoy them. Christians are people who enjoy others, just as David said: "As for the saints in the land, they are the excellent ones, in whom is all my delight" (Ps. 16:3). When we enjoy them, we also praise them. So Paul praises people many times in his epistles. The final chapter of Paul's great theological epistle, Romans 16, mentions thirty-five people by name, and he has something nice to say about nineteen of them! In most of his epistles, he mentions that he thanks God for his readers in his prayers for them. Behind that is the fact that he rejoiced over people. I was able to find twenty-one passages in Paul's epistles where he mentions being joyful over people.

In order to delight in people, we must know the joy of God delighting in us. Five times in the Psalms we are told that God delights or takes pleasure in his people (Pss. 35:27; 41:11; 44:3; 147:11; 149:4). Isaiah says, "The LORD delights in you" (Isa. 62:4; see also Zeph. 3:17). People who know the joy of God delighting in them learn to make delight an important aspect of their lives. This enables them to delight in others, especially their spouses. The result is that we appreciate our spouses and praise them. Those who haven't learned to accept the reality of God delighting in them find it difficult to make delight a major factor in their approach to life. This is a spiritual problem that needs to be corrected.

So praise comes out of joy. But it also increases our joy. When you express appreciation to a person, you are completing the cycle of enjoyment that began with that person's praiseworthy act and proceeded to your appreciation of it. The cycle of joy is completed when we express our appreciation in praise. C. S. Lewis says concerning our call to praise God, "I think we delight to praise what we enjoy because the praise not merely expresses but completes the enjoyment; it is its appointed consummation."[5]

Further, the exercise of telling good things about our spouses helps us to realize afresh their good points. This enables us to grow in our appreciation of them. This, in turn, brightens the relationship in a unique way because we are recognizing the worth of our spouses. So praise gives new levels of joy to the giver and to the receiver. As joy is such an important Christian value, it is no surprise that praise is also a very important Christian practice.

The biblical book Song of Solomon consists of songs of praise from a husband to his wife and a wife to her husband. One of its key teachings is that we study our spouses, meditate on what we see, and express the fruit of our meditation to our spouses in the form of praises. Here is a sample: the husband says: "How beautiful you are, my darling! Oh, how beautiful! Your eyes are doves" (1:15 NIV). The wife responds, "How handsome you are, my beloved! Oh, how charming! And our bed is verdant" (v. 16 NIV).

When I was a student at Fuller Theological Seminary, a popular Christian author, Charlie Shedd, spoke at chapel. It happened to be his twenty-fifth wedding anniversary that day, and his wife was also there. He said that in the twenty-five years he had been married, he had made it a point to compliment his wife at least once each day and to find at least one new thing to compliment her about each week. It is amazing to me how profuse we South Asians are in public praise over the radio and in speeches, but how little we praise people in personal conversation. This lack is particularly found in the home. Sometimes people say, "She knows that I appreciate her, so I don't need to keep telling her." My response is that when there is too much salt in the food, we are sure to point it out, even though she knows it!

So a good way to express our love to our spouses and children is to praise them. Our children will go into a competitive world that can bring a lot of hurt to them. It is amazing how children can hurt each other in school. We cannot shield our children from all of those blows, but we can give them a warm, accepting home environment that communicates to them that they are significant despite what they hear in the outside world. The same can be said of the parents. They often experience competition, jealousy, backbiting, and hurt in their workplaces and even in their churches.

What a relief it is to be able to come back to a home where there is acceptance and appreciation!

Conclusion

We will discuss more about joy in chapter 11 when we talk about children needing to have fun and about happy family traditions. But for now, I urge you to labor to make your home a joyful place. That is a pleasant goal toward which to labor!

7

Disappointment and Pain

A friend of mine who was a regional director of Youth for Christ in the United States told me several years ago that he felt that marriage seminars might be contributing to the high divorce rates among Christians. He said that the seminars presented marriage in such a positive light that people left them with high expectations. When those expectations were not achieved by the couples, they experienced deep disappointment. They tended to think that it was impossible to experience the Christian ideal of a good marriage in their relationships. Therefore, they concluded that their marriages were not God's will, and they split up.

In the Bible, however, there are many stories of unhappy families among God's great people. Hosea had a wife who was a serial adulterer. The family of Jesus thought that he was mad. And the good King Josiah was succeeded by his sons Jehoiakim and Zedekiah, who were bad kings.[1]

No Such Thing as a Perfect Home

In fact, there is no such thing as a perfect marriage or a perfect home. Every family struggles with conflicts, misunderstandings, and hurts. This is why patience is such an important virtue in Christianity. In a book I wrote on love based on 1 Corinthians 13, I had to devote four of the nineteen chapters to the topic of patience.[2] That's how important patience is to a loving life. It is a theme that occurs often in the New Testament. The noun (*hupomonē*) and the verb (*hupomenō*), which have to do with "endurance," appear thirty-two and fourteen times respectively in connection with Christian behavior. The noun (*makrothumia*) and the verb (*makrothumeō*), which have to do with "patience" or "longsuffering," appear nine and six times respectively in connection with Christian behavior. This yields a total of sixty-one occurrences of those terms.

Any happily married couple would tell you that they have faced many difficult challenges that required immense patience and that they continue to live with such challenges. Every Christian has weaknesses and often makes mistakes. Talking to teachers in a passage about the tongue, James says, "We all stumble in many ways" (James 3:2). John says, "If we say we have no sin, we deceive ourselves, and the truth is not in us" (1 John 1:8). Only God is without sin and absolutely perfect. If we expect our family members to be perfect, we put a terrible burden on them. Parents often look on helplessly as they try to understand what has happened to their "perfect child" since he or she became a teenager. I felt that my children's teenage years made me an expert in desperate praying!

At some point, every Christian family will encounter experiences of sickness, conflict, heartache, sorrow, deprivation, disappointment, and failure. So everyone must become skilled in exercising patience. This is a task to which we give ourselves with dedication. Most Christian homes could experience joy in the midst of their pain—joy that would finally overcome the pain. However, there are some Christian homes where the pain lingers and takes away joy, and these homes are characterized by deep distress.

Family Pain

The families of Christian leaders experience pain in many forms. Let me mention a few examples.

I heard the very sad story of the pastor of a rapidly growing church in the United States whose secretary accused him of attempting to have an affair with her. The church believed the secretary, and he had to leave the ministry, with great shame coming to him and his family. Several years later, the secretary confessed that it was she who had wanted to have an affair with him and that he had resisted her advances. What she had said earlier was an angry response to being rejected by him. But because of that response, he was out of the ministry in shame for many years.

One of my dearest friends and colleagues, Suri Williams, who had a wonderful ministry and helped nurture many leaders for the church in Sri Lanka, was hit by Alzheimer's disease in his mid-sixties. He progressively deteriorated to a situation of utter helplessness. His faithful wife, who is a wonderful Christian, has the sorrow of living with a person who is no longer the loving husband she knew for more than three decades.

Benjamin Breckinridge Warfield (1851–1921) was professor of theology at Princeton Theological Seminary for about thirty-four years and is one of the few early twentieth century theologians who is still frequently quoted today. Shortly after his marriage, he went to Europe with his wife, Annie. There the young couple was caught in a violent thunderstorm. Mrs. Warfield was severely traumatized by this, and for the rest of her life—almost forty years—she was a semi-invalid. During this period, Warfield rarely left home for more than two hours at a time. He almost never left the city of Princeton. His student J. Gresham Machen, who later became a famous New Testament scholar, records, "Dr. Warfield used to read to her during certain definite hours every day." He did not get involved in meetings and other activities during a time of great theological turmoil in his Presbyterian denomination. But his brilliant theological writings had a huge impact upon the church.[3]

Likewise, the wife of William Carey, the great missionary to India, went insane after their infant son died, and he had to live with her very difficult behavior for many years.

We know that no one ever fully recovers from the death of a family member—whether it is a child, a sibling, a spouse, or a parent. For the rest of their lives, they live with a hollow place of pain and sorrow in their hearts. There is a sense in which the sting of death will be fully taken away only at the coming resurrection, for which we longingly wait (1 Cor. 15:51–57).

Many people have told me of the loneliness they are experiencing because their spouses do not understand them or the work they are passionate about. The following description of Abraham Lincoln's wife may surprise you:

> She pushed Lincoln relentlessly to seek high public office; she complained endlessly about poverty; she overran her budget shamelessly, both in Springfield and in the White House; she abused servants as if they were slaves (and ragged on Lincoln when he tried to pay them extra on the side); she assaulted him on more than one occasion (with firewood, with potatoes); she probably once chased him with a knife through their backyard in Springfield; and she treated his casual contacts with attractive females as a direct threat, while herself flirting constantly and dressing to kill.[4]

Aiden W. Tozer has been called a twentieth-century prophet. His prophetic insights were used by God to alert the church to many forgotten Christian truths, such as the priority of worship and of spirituality, and the need to be radically committed to God without compromising with the world. However, Tozer did not have a good model of a husband and father in his growing-up years. Though he read widely, he seems to have had a blind spot when it came to knowledge of family responsibilities. His faithful wife, Ada, fulfilled her role as a pastor's wife admirably. But her husband made decisions that affected his family members without consulting them and did not give his wife enough funds to run the family.

Fortunately, Ada did not turn bitter; and though she suffered from financial struggles, loneliness, and a lack of warmth from her husband, she never tried to turn her children against their father.[5] After Tozer died, she married Leonard Odam. When people lovingly inquired about her happiness, she would say: "I have never been happier in my life. Aiden loved Jesus Christ, but Leonard Odam loves me."[6] Tozer was a good and godly man who had a huge influence for good in the church. I am still challenged and nourished when I read his writings. But he was a poor husband and father.

Then there is the painful experience of Christian leaders whose children rebelled against their parents and their God. Many of these parents are as good as any other. They did the right things, but their children went astray. While the Bible does teach that children often carry on the sins of their parents, it also teaches that parents should not be blamed for the sins of their children (Deut. 24:16). Ultimately, children are responsible for their actions, and some, even from the best homes, choose to go the wrong way. Jesus was the greatest of all disciplers, but one disciple betrayed him and committed suicide in bitter remorse. Many great and godly figures of biblical history, such as Abraham, Isaac, Jacob, Aaron, Samuel, David, Josiah, and Jotham, had children who rejected the ways of their parents. This story has been repeated countless times in the history of the church.

I suppose the greatest pain comes from sexual unfaithfulness. How much of that we have seen recently! Often it is the Christian leader who strays. Some of these marriages have been saved through the healing grace of God, though the spouses went through immense pain. But others have ended in divorce. The Bible does not recommend divorce, but acknowledges that sometimes it is inevitable given the hardness of heart of one or both spouses (Matt. 19:8). The immense pain of divorce is known only by those who have experienced it. Some devoted Christians, who attempt to repair their marriages with much effort, prayer, and guidance from others, are finally forced to give in to divorce because of the refusal of their spouses to come to reconciliation.

Frustration, Groaning, Patience, and God's Presence[7]

Let's now look at the pain of families from a biblical perspective. We will look to Romans 8 for guidance here.

Frustration

The Bible teaches that frustration is an inevitable part of life in a fallen world. At the fall, "the creation was subjected to futility ["frustration," NIV], not willingly, but because of him who subjected it, in hope" (Rom. 8:20). So things go wrong. We get sick, we make errors of judgment, we sin, and we face problems from both within and outside the family. But the frustration has an element of "hope" in it. This hope is the final glorious liberation of creation. The creation is eagerly expecting this, and God's children will have a key role in it: "For the creation waits with eager longing for the revealing of the sons of God" (v. 19; see also vv. 21, 23).

Groaning

Until the glorious liberation of creation with the revealing of God's children, the creation will be groaning: "For we know that the whole creation has been groaning together in the pains of childbirth until now" (v. 22). Believers also will groan: "And not only the creation, but we ourselves, who have the firstfruits of the Spirit, groan inwardly as we wait eagerly for adoption as sons, the redemption of our bodies" (v. 23). We have a taste of heaven that Paul calls "the firstfruits of the Spirit," but now we struggle with various kinds of frustration. Our response to these is to groan. The groaning is tinged with the hope of final redemption, so it is called groaning as in the pains of childbirth. A mother in labor groans in great pain, but she knows that this pain will soon be over with the joyous birth of a child.

Learning to groan is a key aspect of the Christian response to problems. The Bible gives us permission to express our pain. We find that over one-third of the Psalms are laments in which

God's faithful servants groan about their problems. Jeremiah, who has been called "the weeping prophet," often described his pain in agonizing language (Jer. 9:1–9; 15:10–21; 20:7–10). Mature Christians, then, have learned to express their pain in groaning, sighing, weeping, and whatever else may be appropriate.

Commitment is one of the hardest features of the Christian lifestyle for twenty-first century believers to adopt. People today have grown used to avoiding suffering and pain, and so, instead of staying on in difficult relationships, they quit and go elsewhere. Today, when problems arise, Christians leave their churches or organizations for others; they leave their jobs, their small groups, and their friends. They haven't learned to suffer in order to keep their commitments. Some approach marriage with the same attitude. When they have problems with their spouses, they quit their marriages.

Those who have learned to groan do not quit that easily. In fact, groaning can prevent quitting. If you know that pain is normal to a relationship, you will not opt out when troubles come. Instead, you will express your pain, knowing that suffering is an essential part of Christianity. You have learned to live with pain and even have joy in the midst of pain. In a book titled *Creative Suffering*, Paul Tournier, who is regarded as the father of contemporary Christian counseling, talks about the sorrow he experienced over the death of his father when he was two years old, that of his mother when he was five years old, and then the death of his wife. He says: "The human heart does not obey the rules of logic: it is constitutionally contradictory. I can truly say that I have a great grief and that I am a happy man."[8] That's how mature Christians behave: they are happy people even when they are living with great grief.

Patience

Paul says in Romans 8:23 that we "groan inwardly as we wait eagerly for adoption as sons, the redemption of our bodies." Things are going to get better, a lot better, one day. Because of that hope,

Paul says, we exercise patience: "But if we hope for what we do not see, we wait for it with patience" (v. 25). I have already mentioned how important patience is to the Christian life. The word used here (*hupomenō*) "denotes not so much a quiet acceptance as a positive endurance (cf. NASB, 'perseverance'). It is the attitude of the soldier who in the thick of the battle is not dismayed but fights on stoutly whatever the difficulties."[9] Later, Paul says, "And we know that for those who love God all things work together for good" (v. 28). If God is working to do something good even through a difficulty, we must join with him and work toward the good that he is going to do. Christians are not fatalists who say, "This is God's will, I must bear it." Instead we say, "God is sovereign over this situation also, so I must work with him to arrive at his good wish for this situation."

Despite the terrible pain of having an unfaithful wife, Hosea did not give up on God. And through his painful experience, he was able to understand God's undying love and patience for his rebellious people. Likewise, the great British Methodist preacher W. E. Sangster was told he was dying of progressive muscular atrophy when he was in his prime as a preacher. His voice was one of the first things that he lost. He made four resolutions when he found out how serious his sickness was. They were: "(1) I will never complain; (2) I will keep the home bright; (3) I will count my blessings; (4) I will try to turn it to gain."[10] He kept himself busy until he died. His last book was written with two fingers and was sent to the publisher one or two days before he died.[11]

It has been said that "The long years of dealing with his tempestuous wife helped prepare [Abraham] Lincoln for handling the difficult people he encountered as president."[12] John Piper comments that "a whole nation benefited from his embracing the pain," because, thanks to this quality, Lincoln "could work so effectively with the rampant egos who filled his administration."[13] So we don't give up when there are problems in our family life. We work till the good comes from it.

God's Presence

Another thing that helps us work amid hardship is the knowledge that God is with us. Paul talks a lot about this in Romans 8. In two powerful sections, he explains how nothing can separate us from the love of Christ (vv. 35, 38–39). With this love, we do not have to be bitter. Circumstances may be terrible and our family members may do wicked things to us, but God's love is greater.

My favorite verse about this in Romans 8 is verse 26: "Likewise the Spirit helps us in our weakness. For we do not know what to pray for as we ought, but the Spirit himself intercedes for us with groanings too deep for words." The Greek word translated as "helps" is a compound formed by the joining of three different words. It literally means "takes share in." This is how a famous New Testament scholar, A. T. Robertson, describes this word: "The Holy Spirit lays hold of our weakness along with us and carries his part of the burden facing us as if two men were carrying a log, one at each end."[14] The idea is that the Spirit comes near to us and shares our burden with us. So real is his sharing that when he intercedes for us, he does so "with groanings too deep for words." Earlier, Paul said that we groan. Now he is saying that the Spirit identifies with us so much that our groanings become his own. He groans with us.

People may not understand, but God does, and he comes to us and identifies with us in our pain. He knows what our pain is because he bore it on the cross. Not only did he take on our sin on the cross, but he also took on our pain and sorrow. Isaiah prophesies, "Surely he has borne our griefs and carried our sorrows" (Isa. 53:4). A Christian lady whose husband was abusing her with very bad language suddenly realized that people had said the same things to Jesus. In a mysterious way, she felt close to God. She was experiencing the fellowship of sharing in Christ's sufferings (Phil. 3:10; see NASB). She was suffering as Christ did, and she knew that Christ identified with her in her pain.

In my younger days, I used to sing in Christian meetings, and I often sang a song that I regard as my personal testimony song. The words and music were written by an evangelist named Charles F. Weigle (1871–1966). Weigle spent most of his life as an itinerant evangelist and gospel songwriter. One day, after returning home from an evangelistic crusade, he found a note left by his wife of many years. The note said she had had enough of an evangelist's life and that she was leaving him. This was so difficult for Weigle that he was paralyzed in terms of ministry for the next several years. There were even times when he contemplated suicide. There was the terrible despair that no one really cared for him anymore. Gradually, his faith was restored and he once again became active in Christian ministry. He wrote the song "No One Ever Cared for Me Like Jesus" as a summary of his past tragic experience.[15]

> I would love to tell you what I think of Jesus
> since I found in Him a friend so strong and true;
> I would tell you how He chang'd my life completely—
> He did something that no other friend could do.
>
> *Chorus:* No one ever cared for me like Jesus;
> there's no other friend so kind as He;
> no one else could take the sin and darkness from me—
> O how much He cared for me! . . .
>
> Ev'ry day He comes to me with new assurance,
> more and more I understand His words of love;
> but I'll never know just why He came to save me,
> till someday I see His blessed face above.[16]

Over the years, I have sung a lot of songs, but I do not think any have moved people as much as this one. I have heard that a prisoner converted on death row requested that he be allowed to sing this song just before he was executed. That was the last thing he did on earth.

Weigle went through an extended period of what might be called "the dark night of the soul." But finally God won through, and Weigle found that Jesus was with him and was sufficient for his daily need. So much eternal good has come to many people through a song that came out of an evangelist's bitter marital experiences.

Accept Biblical Truth

When we face family crises, it is important for us to accept what the Bible says: that God is lovingly with us in our pain and that he is turning it to good. Paul says, "*We know* that for those who love God all things work together for good" (Rom. 8:28). He had accepted by faith the truth that God turns things into good. With such a belief, we can hope in the midst of the gloom and experience the nearness of God because we have an attitude of faith that opens us to experiencing God.

When I stepped down from my role as Sri Lankan national director of Youth for Christ after thirty-five years to take on another role as teaching director, the board gave me three months of leave. My wife and I planned to travel during that time. She had never visited our neighboring nation, India. We planned to visit as semitourists, preaching a little and touring a lot. We planned a trip to the United States also. However, just before this leave period started, while I was in Northern Ireland, my wife called to say that she had cancer. She had taken some tests, and the doctor had been almost sure it was not cancer, so this news shocked me. I cut short the trip, but it was going to be four days before I got home.

It was summertime, and I was staying in a home close to the sea. I was free that evening, so I spent the whole evening on the beach with my Bible (in my phone) and the Lord. I came home, did some preparation, and then went to bed. I did not want to sleep on that bed. I wanted to be home! I began to weep. Suddenly the thought hit me that I was crying to God. He was there with me and he would be with us during this whole ordeal. That experience shaped my approach to the cancer. The thought that came to me often was, "Where would we be without Jesus?"

We had to cancel our travel plans. Instead, during my three-month leave, I spent most of the time at home. We put a small table in our bedroom and I spent time there writing a book on love![17] Usually at Christmastime, I preach a lot. This time, I hardly preached. But I think it was one of my happiest Christmases ever.

The cancer was not an easy experience for us. The experience of chemotherapy was particularly difficult to endure. That was followed by twenty-five rounds of radiation therapy. The treatments seem to have left my wife weaker than before the cancer. Four years later, however, she continues to be clear of the cancer, even though she had a rather virulent attack. And we can see many blessings that God has given us through that difficult time in our lives. But the key was the knowledge that God was with us and was working something good out of this crisis.

In our case, we finally saw clear solutions to our problems. But sometimes that doesn't happen. Some people are not healed of their cancers. Some marriages of good Christians end in divorce. Some weaknesses in our spouses do not change this side of heaven. I have found that my annoying weaknesses are getting worse as I get older, requiring my wife to exercise greater patience. But whether the problems are solved in the way we hope or not, the principles from Romans 8 that I have expounded in this section can always be applied to our lives. First, we must recognize that frustration is a part of life, and so, second, we have the freedom to groan and express our pain. Third, we exercise patience in actively trusting that God will turn every situation into good. Fourth, throughout our time of pain, we experience God's presence, helping us, identifying with us, and comforting us. Fifth, we must accept these four facts and apply them to our lives in faith.

Some Things Can Be Changed

In this chapter, I have talked a lot about problems that cannot be changed and that need to be endured with patience. But some problems *can* be changed. In the journey to a solution, couples may need to get help from a trusted person—such as a pastor, a counselor, or a lay Christian leader—who has had experience in helping such couples.

Most of the staff and volunteers in our Youth for Christ ministry and most of the members of my church are first-generation Christians. They have not had models of Christian family life, and many come from very dysfunctional homes ravaged by alcohol. During their first few years of marriage, they usually encounter major problems. Some come to us senior folk for help. We try to help them understand their spouses and give some advice about modifications they need to make in their attitudes and behaviors. They usually come to realize that their problems are not as insurmountable as they thought. I have seen several such couples, who began their lives together with much turbulence, end up having happy families.

Sometimes couples find it difficult to adjust sexually. This might be because of past experiences that have given them confused attitudes toward sex. Those who have been abused sexually can be repulsed by sex or inflamed with too much sexual desire. Those in the latter group can end up living promiscuous lives, partly because of the desire and partly because they feel they have no purity left to protect. Such people can be helped to experience healing and purity through the grace of Christ mediated through a pastor or counselor. Those who have wrong attitudes toward sex can be brought to realize the biblical approach to sex and sexuality as something beautiful that we are intended to enjoy. Some may be having physically painful sexual relations, and the pain can be alleviated through a simple operation by a surgeon. Many couples have missed the joy of sexual love for unnecessarily long periods because they did not realize the cause of the pain and that a doctor could help alleviate it.

Angry and unhappy people, whose temper is ruining their families, can be led to find the root of their abnormal anger and brought to healing from it. I have worked with people who had deep wounds from childhood (often through the unkindness of a father), but, through counseling, were led to healing prayer and to forgiving the ones who caused the pain. They have seen release and relative freedom from temper tantrums.

David Seamands talks about a young minister who came to see him with his wife. He was having problems getting along with others, especially his wife and family. He was continually criticizing her. Even his sermons were harsh and judgmental. Seamands writes, "He was working out all of his unhappiness on other people."

At the beginning of his interview with Seamands, "he met trouble like a real man: he blamed it on his wife!" But after a while, the painful root of his problem came to light. He had been stationed in Korea while serving in the U.S. armed forces. He spent two weeks of holiday ("R and R") time in Tokyo. "During that leave, walking the streets of Tokyo, feeling empty, lonely, and terribly homesick, he fell into temptation and went three or four times to a prostitute." He could not forgive himself and did not have the assurance that God had forgiven him. He returned home to marry his fiancée, but because of his anger with himself, he was not able to accept her love. He was living in what A. W. Tozer called "the perpetual penance of regret." However, the story has a beautiful ending: the minister accepted God's forgiveness, then received forgiveness from his wife and from himself.[18]

It is sad that many couples with serious problems delay seeking help. While counseling and pastoral care are not solutions to all problems, these can help many people find release from their burdens or grace to endure them.

Persevering Prayer

It goes without saying that the most important thing that one can do when he or she has family problems is to pray. I wrote about this in the first chapter, where I gave the example of Monica, who prayed for her wayward son, Augustine, who was converted shortly before she died. Ruth Bell Graham (Billy Graham's wife), who knew the pain of loving and praying for two wayward sons, wrote a powerful book called *Prodigals and Those Who Love Them*. She points to the prayer of Jesus for his disciples and gives excerpts that form a good summary of the prayers we can pray for wayward children:

> Holy Father, keep through Thine own name those whom Thou has given me. . . . I pray not that thou shouldest take them out of the world, but that Thou shouldest keep them from evil. . . . Sanctify them through Thy truth: Thy word is truth. . . . Father, I will that they also whom Thou has given me, be with me where I am.[19]

I have heard the story of a man whose wife left him, and he had to divorce her. But he never gave up hoping for reconciliation with her. He would regularly walk around the block where she lived, praying for her and for reconciliation. After five years, they were reunited in marriage. Sometimes the prayers of parents for their wayward children see their fruition only after the parents die. Sometimes siblings who are angry with each other are reunited only at the funeral of the mother who was heartbroken over their disunity.

There is a Greek word group in the New Testament that has the idea of "to persist obstinately in."[20] The verb (*proskartereō*) is used five times (Acts 1:14; 2:42, 46; Rom. 12:12; Col. 4:2) and the noun (*proskarterēsis*) once (Eph. 6:18) in connection with prayer. People used to refer to this kind of prayer as prevailing prayer. We must not give up praying; we must persevere!

Don't Let Problems Detract from Nurturing the Family

You may have heard of high-profile couples who had a huge problem with a child, such as a kidnapping or a serious illness, then divorced once the crisis was over. In each case, they gave so much energy to their child's problem that they neglected nurturing their relationship with each other. Usually the couple had serious problems even before the crisis, but the crisis precipitated their disunity until they lost any desire to live with each other.

Everyone in the family needs to be nurtured all the time. Sometimes parents with serious problems with a child, such as severe epilepsy, blindness, autism, hyperactivity, or rebellion, can become severely drained as a result of their response to the problem. They can neglect their own physical, emotional, and spiritual health, and they can neglect each other and other children they have. This can result in serious problems within the family. When instructions about the use of oxygen masks are given on airplane flights, the instructor always tells people with children to fix their masks first and then fix those of the children. Parents need to be healthy and strong in order to help their children.

We must alert parents who have such problems to the dangers of neglecting their own lives and their relationships with their spouses. We must do whatever we can to reduce their pressure. We can free parents off and on and take over some of their responsibilities (such as babysitting) so that they can have a relaxing time away. We can cover these families with special prayers for them. I have a friend with an autistic child, and I have taken it as a personal calling to pray for that family almost daily, especially for grace for the mother. This family lives in another country, but I believe I am reducing their load and increasing the grace being showered on them through my regular prayers for them.

Conclusion

Let me conclude this chapter by going back to a theme I have stressed throughout this book. Nothing must distract us from building our marriages and families. We face many challenges—sickness, weaknesses, misunderstanding, enemies, financial reversals, rebellious children, sexual temptations, and in-law problems. But none of these must get in the way of nurturing our relationships at home. God is committed to our marriages and families. He wants them to be happy and holy, and will give us all the help we need. This gives us confidence to battle for our marriages and families. But we must give top priority to our families and to dealing with the problems that they face.

8

Unity

The Bible often talks of the need for Christians in the church to be united. Paul tells the Philippians, "Complete my joy by being of the same mind, having the same love, being in full accord and of one mind" (Phil. 2:2). Acts presents the early church as being united in this way (Acts 4:32). When disunity arose, the church took urgent steps to restore unity (Acts 6:1–6; 15:1–29). If such unity is the model for church life, how much more important must it be for family life? The Bible has much to say about this unity in the church and in the family.

Unity in Diversity

First Corinthians 12 presents the church as a body that experiences unity amid diversity. This is true in marriage also. When God made humans, he made each one different, thus adding variety and color to life on earth. Our Muslim friends find it difficult to understand why four different portraits of Christ are needed in the Bible. The four Gospels reflect the unique personalities, styles, and emphases of Matthew, Mark, Luke, and John. In the book of Acts, we see Peter, Stephen, and Paul using different preaching styles. Today we have different forms of church government, with each claiming biblical support; likewise, there are different styles of worship and of raising funds. And devout students of the Bible sometimes come up with different interpretations of the same texts. God loves variety.

But in Christianity, within that variety, there is a unity of purpose—to live a life that is pleasing to God. A quote about unity amid diversity in the church, which has been attributed to several Christian leaders from the past, beginning with Augustine, is very helpful to family life as well. It says, "In essentials, unity; in nonessentials, liberty; in all things, charity." Large-hearted people are willing to let others follow their tastes, though they may not choose the same ways. This attitude is very important in the home, enabling each family member to blossom to his or her fullest.

Most men in Sri Lanka like to watch sports and politics on TV more than their wives do. And so long as this is not done to such an excessive extent as to hurt the family, a large-hearted wife can release her husband to enjoy some sports or political programs. She may even develop an interest in these things because of her love for her husband. While many men are developing a love for cooking programs on TV, more Sri Lankan women enjoy these than men. The men can gladly release their wives to watch these programs and help out by taking on some of their responsibilities during those times.

A husband and wife may have different ideas about how a home should be decorated and what colors the walls should be painted. Differences may emerge in preferences for foods, for places to go on holidays, for gifts to purchase for loved ones, for getting up early or late in the morning, and for a host of other things. Usually neither option breaks a moral principle. These have to do with tastes. Big-hearted people can give in to the will of others without acting immature and insisting on their way.

Much has been written about what an asset Ruth Bell Graham was to the life and ministry of her husband, Billy. Theirs was a happy marriage. But Ruth often said about her marriage that she and Billy were "happily incompatible." Their daughter Gigi Graham Tchividjian has said: "They have very different personalities, strengths, ideas, and ways of doing things. But, Mother is fond of saying, 'If two people agree on everything, one of them is unnecessary.'"[1] Though she married a famous Baptist preacher, she never gave up some of her Presbyterian convictions, such as her belief in infant baptism. Ruth and Billy seem to embody the idea that Chuck and Barb Snyder used as the theme of their book *Incompatibility: Still Grounds for a Great Marriage*. The word *Still* was added to the title in the second edition, published eleven years after the first edition.[2]

A key to being happily incompatible is following Paul's advice: "In humility count others more significant [or "better," NLT] than yourselves" (Phil. 2:3). Everyone has something he or she is better at than us. We need to focus on those things rather than the aspects of a person's personality that may annoy us. Christians who look down on their spouses are breaking the biblical model of community life. They need to repent. Paul also says, "Outdo one another in showing honor" (Rom. 12:10). Rather than looking down, we look up to our family members. We are committed to bringing them honor. This means that we discipline ourselves to focus on their strong points and to learn to be patient with their weak points. Yes, this is a discipline. We have a choice as to what we focus on. Love drives us to make the other person's strong points our main focus.

Sometimes we have a hierarchy of values, on the basis of which we consider another inferior to ourselves. For example, a highly educated person who is well aware of political and economic trends in the world may get married to someone with minimal education and little or no interest in politics and the economy. The educated one can be tempted to consider his or her spouse inferior because of this. Those attitudes must be strenuously battled. If the highly educated person looks with an open mind, he or she will see many qualities in the less-educated person that can be greatly admired. This has been my experience in my work with poor, illiterate people. How much they have taught me!

Yet the weaknesses of our family members, especially our spouses, may be difficult to live with. This is why patience is such an important Christian value, especially in family life. We have already said that terms from the two main word groups for "patience" occur sixty-one times in the Greek New Testament. That's how important patience is to the Christian life. Patience is the first characteristic of love mentioned in the long list in 1 Corinthians 13:4–7 and is named as part of the fruit of the Spirit (Gal. 5:22). Because it is a fruit of the Spirit, we know that we can have strength to be patient through the power of the indwelling Spirit. This gives us the confidence to pursue patience and the resolve to apply it when we are annoyed. Because patience is a part of the *agapē* love that we described in chapter 3, we know that we must make a firm decision to be patient when we are tempted to lash out impatiently. God's enabling and our commitment to decide to be patient will take away the barriers to honoring our spouses and children.

What a source of joy it is to know that our spouses, parents, siblings, and children look at us with honor and appreciate our opinions and styles. Even when we argue, we do so in keeping with the characteristic of Christian love, which "does not insist on its own way" (1 Cor. 13:5). Christians are people who have surrendered their wills to God, as we saw in chapter 2. So it is not a big deal for them to adjust in order to accommodate the idiosyncrasies of family members.

Of course, there are some issues about which we cannot afford to remain in disagreement. On such, we must talk and pray until agreement is reached. One of these issues involves children. I know of wives who stopped taking birth-control pills without telling their husbands. They knew that their husbands did not want to have children at that time, but they did. So they got pregnant, knowing that their husbands would have to accept the babies. In chapter 12, we will see how important it is for parents to agree on the way they will discipline their children when they do something wrong.

Husbands and wives also need to be united about how they will spend their money. There will always be nonmajor expenses that do not need spousal agreement. But for major decisions, agreement is necessary. How much will they give for God's work and for the needy? What major appliances will they purchase? In Sri Lanka, I know of several Christian leaders whose wives took loans for personal expenses without their husbands' knowledge. When the husbands learned of it, their reactions were very unpleasant, and those marriages suffered serious blows to their unity.

On Sri Lankan television, we often see spouses manipulating each other in order to persuade them to agree to something. Sometimes one is outwitted and has no alternative but to agree to the spouse's request. Such concessions are not made wholeheartedly. While the person who got what he or she wanted is satisfied, the unity of the family is strained. Christian spouses "walk in the light" with each other (1 John 1:7). One manipulating the other to get something violates this biblical principle. Christians must express their disapproval of actions or plans of their spouses if they are unhappy with them. But they do that out of a self that is surrendered to God. So they are willing to crucify self, to change their minds, and then support something they may not have liked at first.

Conversation Deepens Unity

In the chapter on joy, I mentioned how Charlie Shedd said on his twenty-fifth wedding anniversary that he had made it his practice to compliment his wife every day. On his thirtieth anniversary, he wrote an article entitled "Talk! Talk! Talk!" His point was that a key to a happy marriage is couples talking regularly about the things of God, especially things that they get from the Scriptures.[3] After saying that the words he was commanding the Israelites should be on their hearts, Moses said, "You shall teach them diligently to your children, and shall talk of them when you sit in your house, and when you walk by the way, and when you lie down, and when you rise" (Deut. 6:7). This is a description of a home centered on the Word of God.

Some couples talk almost exclusively about problems, opportunities, decisions, and other practical issues facing the family. These things are important. If couples have no time to talk about issues they face, their relationship will soon grow distant. When the family faces an issue, time must be separated for serious conversation. But a happy home is not founded upon issues the family faces; it is founded upon God and his ways. So the Word of God must figure prominently in the conversation in the family. If the challenges the family faces are most important, then when these take a wrong turn, the family will lose its security and joy.

We affirm that God is the head of our home when we talk about what we read in the Bible for our devotions that day or about some insight we got from a Christian book or Sunday's sermon. We do so when we climax a conversation about an issue in prayer. We do so when we see something on the TV and discuss whether what we saw is in harmony with God's Word. We do so when we share testimonies and stories of the blessings God has given us or others. There is deep satisfaction in talking about eternal things found in the Bible. It buttresses the truth that God is the foundation of our homes.

Of course, topics related to the Word of God are not the only things that a couple talks about. It is very important to talk about practical matters relating to the running of the house. When the children are small, the wife may have a tough day coping with their care. The husband comes home tired after a heavy day of work and is in no mood to talk. But it is absolutely essential for the wife to talk about her frustrating experiences of the day. If she is deprived of such opportunities, she can end up bitter. The important goal of parents being united about the discipline of their children is also achieved through conversation.

When our children lived at home, my wife and I had a rule that we would not turn the television on during mealtimes. After they grew up and left, we decided that, if possible, we would have our dinner at the time of the news on TV. I am very interested in current affairs. My wife is also interested, but not as much as I am. She understands that it is a good thing for her to know at least a little about things that interest me. So I am able to explain to her the backgrounds or other issues relating to the events being described. Her willingness to talk to me about the things that interest me is an important aspect of our unity. Usually, after dinner, we wash the dishes together (we do not have a dishwasher). This also gives us opportunity for relaxed conversation.

Implied in what is said above is the truth that a husband and his wife are good friends who like being with each other. We can easily become annoyed with our family members. Because the push to act and put on a show is less strong in the home, we can give vent to our annoyances and make our home an unhappy place. One of the things that cures such impatience is long conversation times. Friendship between spouses is usually forged through their determined decision to work hard at conversation. When tension arises in relationships, long chats about the issues help resolve it.

It is amazing how many couples talk for long hours before they are married, but talk so much less afterward. Sometimes, in our busyness, we can neglect conversation without realizing it. If this happens, the one who notices it must tell his or her spouse about it as soon as possible. Sometimes when I think that my wife and I are doing fine as a couple, she asks me something like this: "Do you know that we haven't had a long chat for about two weeks?" I have been so busy that I have not realized this serious neglect on my part. I am jolted back to reality and forced to take some immediate steps to repair the situation. When a couple realizes that they have neglected conversing with each other, they should regard it as an emergency requiring immediate action, even though it may be quite inconvenient to take such action.

Sometimes couples spend little time with each other because it is practically impossible to do so. When I travel abroad, even though my wife and I communicate many times a day, usually through WhatsApp, a distancing takes place because of the physical separation. So when I return home, I usually leave the next day completely free so that we can "get caught up." When I have had to fit something in on that day, I have always sensed that it has not been good for us. Creating space in our schedules for talking is something we must do with consistency and determination.

H. Norman Wright has presented a scenario that occurs in many marriages. He says, "Often a man builds his identity through his occupation or profession." Wright notes that the traditional roles of husbands and wives are changing now, with women also pursuing professions and careers. But it is still true that husbands are the primary income-earners in many marriages. The husband marries at about the same time he is trying to establish himself in his line of work. While his wife is looking for intimacy, he is busy finding his identity through his vocation. Frustration may occur as a result. Wright says, "It can be described as identity versus intimacy!" Once the children come, the wife (disappointed by the lack of affection from her husband) concentrates on showing affection to her children.

Then the scenario shifts. Wright says: "Many husbands in their forties realize they have reached the end of the line for upward progress in their work. There is nowhere else to go, so their goals begin to change. They may turn back to their wives with a desire to build intimacy." By then, however, the children are grown up and the wife is thinking of pursuing her career and educational dreams. She was hurt by her husband's neglect during their crucial first years of marriage, so she does not respond to his desires for intimacy with the intensity he expects.[4] The result can be that they never experience the intimacy they once desired. Couples must be alert to this danger and consciously keep nurturing conversation all through their married lives. In chapter 4, I said that it might be a kind of death for a husband to talk to his wife when he is tired and in no mood for conversation. But he is willing to embrace that "death" in order to give himself up for his wife as Christ did in dying for the church (Eph. 5:25).

Making a determined decision to talk when one does not feel like doing so is a key to a happy marriage. If there is no immediate prospect of time to talk, we must somehow find the time soon. We may need to use our creativity to do this. Two days before I wrote this, my wife and I were caught in a traffic jam. A journey we expected to take a few minutes took us close to an hour. At the end of the journey, I told my wife that it had been a great blessing because we had had an opportunity to chat without any disturbances.

People usually make the time to do what they regard as absolutely essential. If you regard relaxed conversation as absolutely essential, you will somehow make the time for it. Many times in this section, I have said that we must make a conscious decision to talk. Conversation with our spouses is a key aspect of obedience to God. The blessing of such conversation is a deepening union with each other.

Unity about Our Ministries

It is essential that those involved in ministry as volunteers or paid workers talk about their ministries with their spouses. Unmarried people with a passion for ministry should be wary about choosing a spouse who does not share that passion. In the heat of love, one can think that the other will grow to be interested in the ministry. There have been times when this has happened, but we can never be sure that it will. A person thinking about full-time service should be sure that the one he or she hopes to marry senses a corresponding call to be the spouse of a full-time worker.

Because ministry is time consuming, families pay a big price when a member is involved in it. If the others in the family do not have much knowledge of what the person in ministry is doing, it is easy for them to become resentful about the ministry. This can happen even to spouses who have a deep commitment to ministry. There are some things that we cannot share with our family members, such as details of sexual problems encountered by a person we are counseling. But our families need to have some knowledge of the things we do and why they are so important.

We must make sure that we talk to our spouses about our schedules. This is an area in which I have failed often. My wife and I have the habit of going through my datebook regularly so that she can write my key appointments in her datebook. But sometimes this does not happen. As a result, there are times when she does not know about an important, time-consuming program I am going to be involved in. When she finds out, it is a surprise, and she realizes that she needs to make many adjustments to accommodate my schedule. God somehow sees us through, but that is because of his mercy despite all the disqualifying things I do!

Mothers can lose their love for service during the frustrating years of raising infants. Often, ministry wives enjoy being involved in ministry before the children come. When the little ones arrive, a wife may experience a sense of confinement, and she can miss the ministry deeply. The husband needs to keep her informed about what is happening and pray with her about those things. This way, her taste for ministry is not lost.

Couples can also look for ways in which the wife can be involved in service from home. When our children were small, we had needy young women staying with us for short periods of time. A woman living alone may be close to a nervous breakdown, but she can regain health in the environment of a caring home. A woman without a place to live can stay in a home for a short time until her problem is resolved. A youth abused by a father can find a safe haven in a Christian home until more permanent arrangements are made. After the major ethnic riots in Sri Lanka, we opened our home to people of a different race for more than six months because their homes had been burned. Our son was born during this time, and our daughter was three years old. But we remember those busy months as a happy and fulfilling time.

Having people over for meals also keeps the spirit of service alive in the home. You don't need to spend a lot of time preparing an elaborate meal. That can become burdensome. The reason for inviting others is primarily fellowship, not food. Too much emphasis on having the home looking perfect and on cooking a delicious meal puts a burden on a young mother who is caring for little children. But the act of cooking and fellowshiping for the benefit of an outsider helps keep the taste for ministry alive.

If the taste for ministry is maintained through minimal involvement when the children are little, the wife can snap back into a life of ministry outside the home when the children are grown up. Sadly, some wives lose their taste for and excitement over ministry so much that even when they are relatively free, they do not get involved in ministry again. This can become a source of disunity if the husband is still involved. Yet service during difficult times can be overdone. As we look back, we see that some of the assignments we took on when our children were small may have been too difficult on my wife. Fortunately, she came out of them without any serious scars.

It is very important that we do not stereotype spouses and expect them to conform to a pattern that may not be suitable to them. The wife of the founder of Youth for Christ, from whom I took over leadership, was very active in the ministry, and she was a very energetic and much appreciated servant of Christ. My wife's personality and gifts are very different. When we married, I realized that people expected my wife to go to all the public gatherings that it was my duty to attend. But she was not inclined to do that. God gave her a wonderful personal ministry, and a lot of that ministry was in our church. So she was a somewhat atypical YFC director's wife. But we let her fashion her priorities according to her giftedness. Soon it became evident to all that if I had any effectiveness as a leader, my wife had a big part to play in that. The YFC community released her to follow the path God had chosen for her.

It is a favorite pastime of Christians to criticize the spouses of Christian leaders, especially pastors' wives. They compare them with other spouses and conclude that they fall short of the standards expected of them. Sadly, in every church, there are insecure and unhappy people who find fulfillment in criticizing others. We must not let such ungodly people rule our lives. We must protect our spouses from these people and not add to the pain by giving more weight to these criticisms than they deserve. Sometimes people criticize a wife for how untidy her house is. The worst scenario is when her mother-in-law makes this criticism. She is barely surviving the strain of raising her children, and sometimes she is forced to neglect some housekeeping details. Her husband cannot prevent people from criticizing, but he can reduce her pain by comforting her and refusing to join in the criticism. A husband may be tempted to lash out angrily because he is embarrassed by the criticism, but he must not give in to that temptation.

Conclusion

You can see that maintaining unity requires hard work on the part of both husband and wife. This is in accord with Paul's teaching on unity within the church. He urges Christians to be "eager to maintain the unity of the Spirit in the bond of peace" (Eph. 4:3). We do not create this unity. It is "the unity of the Spirit." But we can mess up and blow it. So Paul tells us that we must "maintain" it. This requires urgent action on our part. The verb translated as "eager" (*spoudazō*), when used as it is here (followed by an infinitive), takes the meaning of "to be especially conscientious in discharging an obligation, be zealous/eager, take pains, make every effort, be conscientious."[5] All this points to the urgency with which we follow the call to unity in the church and, by implication, in the family.

9

The Love Fight

In the last chapter, we talked about the urgency of maintaining unity in the family. Yet most healthy families have times when differences emerge, unity is broken, and conflict arises. I have heard couples say that they have never had a conflict in all their years of marriage. I do not want to disbelieve them, but if what they say is true, their marriages are rare exceptions, not the rule. Most spouses experience conflicts, which we might call "love fights."[1] Paul gives some important rules for love fights in Ephesians 4:25–27, and we will follow the guidelines he gives there.

Rule #1: Be Truthful

The first rule for a love fight is, "Be truthful." Paul says, "Therefore, having put away falsehood, let each one of you speak the truth with his neighbor, for we are members one of another" (Eph. 4:25). A result of being members of the same body is that we cannot lie to each other. Problems, disagreements, and annoyances will surely come in the home. We will be tempted to lie to evade unpleasant confrontations. But while one may postpone an unpleasant confrontation, such playacting is not good for the marriage. It erects a barrier that prevents full union between husband

and wife. Usually the unhealed wound opens up in a much more unpleasant confrontation than would have happened if it had been faced right at the start.

Lying is very much a part of many cultures today, and people do not think it is wrong to lie. Sometimes denying wrongdoing is accepted if that avoids shame coming to the family or to the wrongdoer. In fact, some think that admitting to wrongdoing and facing the shame of it is a greater wrong than the wrong act itself. However, as a result of repeated lying, families grow used to living with unresolved issues. Sometimes everyone knows that the father has done something wrong, but everyone pretends that they don't know. A great relief comes to the home when the thick cloud of pretense is cleared by a wrongdoer taking responsibility for his or her actions.

I have seen situations in which the wife refuses to accept that her husband is having an affair, even though almost everyone else knows this is happening. She valiantly defends him in public and revolts against any disciplinary action the church may take against him. While her loyalty to her husband is admirable, it is based on untruth. One can never really hope for deep unity in such a marriage relationship. The husband admitting to the affair may bring extreme pain at first. But God's grace is greater than the biggest sin. If grace is conscientiously applied to that situation, a deep unity can be forged through the pain.

Sometimes people use deceitful methods to persuade their spouses to agree to things the spouses are reluctant to accept. We see this all the time in dramas on television. I talked about this in the previous chapter, giving the example of wives who stopped taking their birth-control pills without the knowledge of their husbands, who were not eager to have children at that time.

Maintaining outward peace by refusing to face up to an issue or securing desired things by deceitful means negatively affects unity. When this happens, a family misses the freedom and joy that come from open, trusting relationships in which the members are "of the same mind, having the same love, being in full accord and of one mind" (Phil. 2:2). You cannot be of one mind if you are not truthful.

Rule #2: Be Angry and Do Not Sin

Next, Paul says, "Be angry and do not sin" (Eph. 4:26a). When someone we deeply love does something wrong or hurtful, our natural reaction is often anger. Sometimes this is called righteous anger. Once, after I finished a sermon on anger, someone challenged me, saying that the phrase "righteous anger" is not found in the Bible. While the exact phrase may not be found, the concept is certainly there. God is presented in the Bible as being angry over the sins of his people. Jesus was angry over the hypocrisy of the scribes and Pharisees. Paul was boiling with anger over the defection of Peter and Barnabas to the side of the circumcision party in Galatia (Gal. 2:11–14). But Paul also says that we must not sin when we are angry.

Let's look at some examples of how we can sin when we are angry during a family love fight. When we are very angry, we can lose control of ourselves and say things that we should not say. So it is best to keep quiet. I jokingly tell my wife that I am glad God gave us teeth, because when I am angry and could say hurtful things to her, I go to my room and grit my teeth instead. (I do not know what I will do when I am old and have no teeth!) Hurtful language goes deep into a person's soul and can continue to affect him or her for years, even after an apology has been made. When we say things in anger, we do not, in our heart of hearts, mean what we say, but the words come out and, like James says, cause havoc like a forest fire (James 3:5).

We sin when we resurrect past transgressions that have been forgiven and put behind us. Describing the blessings of the new covenant, God says, "For I will forgive their iniquity, and I will remember their sin no more" (Jer. 31:34). While God can forget sins, we may not be able to erase the wrongs done against us from our minds completely. But we can act as if the sin never happened. This is one application of Paul's statement that love "keeps no record of wrongs" (1 Cor. 13:5 NIV). The verb used there (*logizomai*) is often found in contexts of financial accounting. Just as a bookkeeper keeps a record of a transaction for future reference, we also can do so with wrongs done to us. Love refuses to do that. When we resurrect past sins, we complicate the battle and take an unfair advantage that may result in us winning the argument but losing our unity with our spouses.

Sometimes great harm has come to the family, for which one spouse has to bear responsibility. The effects are ongoing. For example, careless driving by the husband results in an accident that takes the life of a child. That is a terrible thing to live with. But no matter how hard it may be, a Christian wife strives to not blame her husband. Believing in the power of forgiveness for wrongdoing and in the power of the sovereign God to help them start afresh, she disciplines herself not to bring up the accident, even in a time of serious conflict.

We must never, never, never use physical force on our spouses. I talked about this in chapter 4. When I wrote that, I thought that domestic violence was a serious problem in my part of the world and not so much in the affluent West. Since writing that, I have come to know that it is a problem in the West also. And the church is not exempt from this scourge. Even the slightest use of physical force should be accompanied by deep sorrow, confession, and pleading for forgiveness from the offended party. If force is used once, it likely will be used often after that. Drastic steps should be taken to place controls upon those who lift their hands against their spouses. Having an accountability structure—in which the offending person knows that if he or she does it again, another person will be brought in to intervene and impose discipline—can be a great help here.

One spouse's use of underhanded methods that immediately put the other on the defensive does not befit God's children. When a wife contrasts her husband with her sister's husband, she is bringing about hurt that can be very damaging. People are different, so we must not expect one's behavior to conform to the pattern of another. It is immature, foolish, and unkind to bring up the example of someone else to show the weaknesses of one's spouse.

When one spouse brings up a problem, the other should not accuse him or her of bad motives for doing that. Take the example of a wife who tells her husband, "I prefer that you do not chat with your old girlfriend." The husband could take that as good advice, a helpful reminder to be careful. Or he could honor the advice simply because it is the wish of his beloved wife. I personally believe that it is very good advice to tell someone not to spend too much time with a former girlfriend or boyfriend. However, when the wife says this, the husband might respond angrily with words like these: "Do you think I am a person like that?" "Are you accusing me of having an affair with her?" or "Don't you trust me?" But if he reacts like this, the wife will not want to bring up such issues again. This, of course, means that there will be no opportunity for them to resolve problems when they arise. The couple will move apart.

When our spouses point out faults or dangerous trends in our lives, it can be hard to accept. We may feel humiliated by it. But it can be very health-giving. Speaking about leaders, James says, "For we all stumble in many ways" (James 3:2a). As we are prone to make mistakes, if we are sincere, honorable people, we should welcome all the help we can get to avoid and overcome errors.

Of course, there is a way to bring up an issue. We can do it without being accusatory. For example, when a wife feels that her husband ignores her when he comes home after work, she can angrily accuse him, saying, "You don't love me!" Alternatively, she can say, "I would like if you would spend a little time talking to me when you come back from work." After I had finished preaching on Ephesians 4 one Sunday, a friend told me, "We have outlawed the words *never* and *always* in our family." He meant that statements such as "You never help me" and "You are always hurting me" were taboo in his home.

Four of my five examples of sinning while being angry are related to the use of the tongue. We must be very careful about what we say when we are angry. The prayer of Psalm 141:3 is one that should be prominent in the lives of all sincere Christians: "Set a guard, O LORD, over my mouth; keep watch over the door of my lips!"

Rule #3: Do Not Let the Sun Go Down on Anger

Paul's next rule is, "Do not let the sun go down on your anger" (Eph. 4:26b). He is saying that we should not give up the battle until a resolution to the problem comes. I gave my first wedding sermon exactly a year after I got married. In that sermon, I told the couple that when they had a problem, they should not go to sleep until it was resolved. Some of my friends responded to that sermon by suggesting that after a few more years of marriage, I would learn that what I had preached was not practical. But after thirty-nine years of marriage, I still recommend that! I know problems can be complex and difficult to unravel. But we must not stop grappling for a solution.

There are two exceptions I would make to this rule. The first is that it is unwise to talk about a problem when you are very angry. We just discussed that. The second is that some spouses can be so insecure that they cannot handle confronting unpleasant issues. This is a rare exception, and we can easily judge too soon that our spouses are not able to handle such issues. People with such spouses should pray for them to grow in confidence and trust so that a time will come when they can share freely when there are disagreements. They must be aware that they can abdicate the responsibility to handle unpleasant problems by using the spouse's supposed weakness as an excuse.

Often problems surface in a marriage when one spouse (or both) is very busy. That's when couples tend to neglect each other.

Because of the busyness, the natural tendency is to postpone confronting a problem until the busy period is over. But delaying to confront unity issues can be very dangerous. Jesus underlined the urgency of reconciliation among members of the church in his Sermon on the Mount. He said that if one coming to the temple with a gift remembers that a brother has something against him, he should leave the gift at the altar and be reconciled to the brother, then come back to offer the gift (Matt. 5:23–24). If the need to reconcile with a fellow disciple is so urgent, how much more urgent is the need to reconcile with our own family members!

A couple may need to go on grappling for a solution to a problem until the early hours of the morning. They may go to work the next morning with red eyes from a lack of sleep. But they will go with hearts freed from a huge burden, enjoying unity with the most important person in their lives. Often, especially at a busy time, when spouses tend to neglect each other, God can use a conflict to get the couple back on track as a united pair.

Sadly, some people do not want full resolution to their problems. They find some satisfaction in nurturing the idea that they have been hurt by their spouses. Self-pity is a friend that will not disappoint us if we want to nurture our anger against those who hurt us. Some couples go for days without talking with each other after a conflict. While that is common even among Christians, it is a violation of biblical principles. When we wallow in self-pity, we dampen the flame of love in our hearts. Self-love can hinder our love for our spouses, but genuine love does not rest until complete unity is restored.

Sometimes working for a resolution is delayed because one spouse (or both) wants to establish that the other is a bad person. Because the other person is "bad," they say, it is not possible to work for a resolution. "There is no point," such a spouse says, "in wasting time trying to come to a resolution with such an ungodly person." Taking the "moral high ground" in this way does little to help create a happy family. We come back to a teaching we presented in the last chapter: Christians count others better than themselves (Phil. 2:3). That is our basic approach to people. With this attitude, we will not resort to inaction by saying that the other person is bad.

Rule #4: Give No Opportunity to the Devil

Finally, Paul says, "Give no opportunity to the devil" (Eph. 4:27). When we don't resolve serious disagreements, we can let anger linger in our hearts. This provides an opportunity for Satan to impact us in a way that causes us to end up doing really bad things. The NIV translates this verse as "Do not give the devil a foothold." Satan can enter a little part of our lives when we make ourselves vulnerable to his attacks by nurturing anger. This can lead to more serious problems. Those who keep anger in their hearts will hurt other people sooner or later. The anger may be suppressed, but it will surface when the conditions are right.

An American family therapist, Dr. Sandra D. Wilson, has written a book entitled *Hurt People Hurt People.*[2] She shows how people who are hurt act out of that hurt and end up hurting others. The book also prescribes a way to overcome these hurts. Some of these hurt people may be devoted church members. In fact, in family conflicts, they may be in the right. But because they keep anger in their hearts, they act impatiently with others and end up hurting them. We can call these people "righteous but wicked." They could be the cause for joy leaving Christian homes.

The Aim Is Unity, Not Victory

Sri Lanka endured a civil war for almost thirty years. It ended in 2009. At different times during this war, the rebels and the government forces had significant victories. After the government forces had won a major battle, the president of Sri Lanka, R. Premadasa, went on national television and said that in a war, there are no victors. He meant that Sri Lankans were fighting Sri Lankans, and a victory in such a conflict would not solve the problem. The solution was peace and harmony between all the peoples of Sri Lanka.

In the same way, winning is not the aim of a love fight in a family. That is like winning a small battle in a war without winning the war itself. We can win small battles and still lose the war. Real victory is achieved and the war is won when there is unity, when the home is a happy and harmonious place. Victories in small battles satisfy small people. Big people look at the big picture. So when we are engaged in a love fight, our main desire is for unity, harmony, and love to be restored, and for the problem that caused the fight to be solved. The desire to get what we want or to win the argument is subsumed under the greater desire for family harmony. Those who truly love their spouses want unity more than anything else. When one is satisfied with a petty victory, it is a sign that self-love has overcome Christian love.

Apologizing

Usually when there is a love fight, both parties have failed in some way. One person may deserve the majority of the blame for the problem, but during the fight, it often becomes evident that the other person has also done wrong. Until those responsible for the different problems have apologized, there can be no lasting solution.

The main theme of 1 John 1:5–10 is the necessity of walking in the light. Verses 5, 8 and 10 show that a key aspect of walking in the light is accepting that we have done wrong. According to verse 9, this is expressed by those seeking to walk in the light confessing their sins (to God). Verse 7a brings up the relational aspect of walking in the light: "But if we walk in the light, as he is in the light, we have fellowship with one another." By looking at the context of this verse, we can conclude that it teaches that if we arc to have real fellowship, we must seek to follow God's ways and confess when we fail to do so. Those who are not serious about obeying God and accepting their faults cannot have real Christian fellowship. They may hug, kiss, chat, and laugh, but there is a barrier to real unity.

When I was a teenager, I heard an American missionary in Sri Lanka, Don Rubesh, say, "The four hardest words to say in the home are, 'I'm sorry, I'm wrong.'" A friend once told me, "I have never heard my wife apologize." A lady also told me the same thing about her husband. Unless these people are angels, they surely have reasons to apologize. We all fail to live up to God's perfect standards. Yet it is humiliating to accept that we have done wrong. In shame- and honor-oriented cultures, such as those in Asia and even in the West (especially among minority communities), apologizing is particularly difficult. As noted earlier, some consider the shame of being exposed as having done wrong to be worse than the wrong deed itself. We therefore need to have good reasons for believing that it is worth apologizing.

The most powerful reason for apologizing has to do with the biblical doctrine of grace. Our sin blocks God's grace from coming into our lives. Grace is the most important thing in our lives. If there is anything truly worthwhile in our lives, it comes through grace. Therefore, losing access to grace should be a terrifying thing for a Christian. Our failure to apologize blocks the inflow of grace. Because of this, if we sin against someone, we should want to apologize as soon as we realize what we have done. Our desire for grace gives us the strength to apologize. Those who are afraid to apologize have not understood grace. This makes them so weak that they do not have the strength to apologize.

Another reason for apologizing is that it restores the honor and spiritual freedom of the wrongdoer. Earlier in this chapter, I talked about the thick cloud of pretense that exists in a home where one has done wrong but does not admit to it. A husband or father may be respected and may wield his authority as the head of the home, but that is earthly respect and authority, given by virtue of his position, not because it is deserved. In fact, along with the earthly authority, there may be hidden resentment

against the husband or father. When wrongdoers accept responsibility for their wrongdoing, the thick cloud of pretense lifts and
is replaced by the freedom of openness and respect for those who
acknowledge their sin. Then couples can have real fellowship
with each other. This is the teaching of 1 John 1:7: "But if we
walk in the light, as he is in the light, we have fellowship with
one another, and the blood of Jesus his Son cleanses us from all
sin." We have already seen that the context of that verse shows
that one aspect of walking in the light is admitting that we have
done wrong.

When I was a youth, there was a committee meeting in our
home, hosted by my father. I could hear a heated debate going on
in the meeting. With time, the debate became bitter, with some
unkind and unpleasant things said. Among those who were talking heatedly at the meeting was the highly esteemed and brilliant
Sri Lankan bishop, Lakshman Wickremesinghe. The day after the
meeting, the bishop came to our home to meet my father and to
apologize for the way he had spoken. I have never forgotten that. I
have always held the bishop in high esteem because of that display
of godly humility.

However, our personalities also influence our willingness to
apologize. Some people find it easier to apologize than others.
Usually a love fight ends only after both parties apologize. And
usually it is the same person who apologizes first in each love fight.
This should not be a problem. We must recognize that people
are wired differently. The main thing is that everyone who has
done something wrong apologizes in order to have a complete and
genuine unity. The fact that one person always apologizes first is
not a serious issue.

God Is There

I have described, in the first chapter and elsewhere, how God
influences every aspect of our family lives. This is true of the love
fight also:

- The knowledge that God is greater than the problem and will turn it to good gives us the courage to face up to it honestly and to initiate the dialogue that becomes a love fight.
- The belief that, because God is sovereign and involved in the issue, he will guide us to a solution gives us the perseverance to battle without giving up until a solution is found.
- The realization that God is there with us helps moderate the fight. God is like an umpire controlling the battle. The awareness of his presence and the security it brings prevent us from panicking and acting in rash and foolish ways. His presence prevents us from resorting to violence, to insults, and to harsh and hurtful language. You cannot talk like that if you realize that God is listening. Paul said, "Let the peace of Christ rule in your hearts" (Col. 3:15a). The peace we have because of Christ rules (controls) our behavior and prevents us from going to unhealthy extremes.
- The wonderful forgiveness that God gives us helps us to start anew after we have failed.
- The experience of forgiveness that we enjoy motivates us to forgive the other for the wrong he or she has done.
- Having been forgiven and having forgiven the other, we are able to make a fresh start to the relationship with the past decisively left behind.

Our God is a God who constantly makes things new. When we honestly face up to the problems we have and initiate a dialogue about them using his methods, he is able to use the problems to bring fresh blessings to our lives together. Don't be afraid of confronting unpleasant issues. God is greater than them!

Conclusion

Pragmatism rules so much human interaction today that people don't worry too much about personal relationships, so long as the job gets done. There isn't a strong sense of commitment to people in organizations or even in churches. If someone can't work toward the goals of the organization or church, they just leave and go somewhere else. Sadly, many seem to have allowed this approach to invade family life also. If the family runs "efficiently," the members seem to be satisfied. But the biblical model of community is that of a body—of people who are committed to each other and to living with one heart and mind. If so, we must seriously devote ourselves to implementing this model in family life. It is inefficient and it consumes a lot of time and energy. But the rewards are security, deep love, and trust in the relationships between family members. That is a goal worth paying a huge price to achieve.

10

Delighting in Children

Our children are growing up in a world, unlike the world their parents grew up in, where the basic convictions of right and wrong have been blurred. Every generation has had its share of evil attractions. But today, moral relativism is a value that is so strongly held that those holding to traditional values of right and wrong are considered to be out of sync with contemporary culture. One of the best ways to combat this problem is to create a home atmosphere of general well-being and acceptance, so that children see that the values held by their families do indeed produce the best environment for a fulfilling life. In this and the next chapter, we will look at features of a healthy family environment for children to grow up in.

Children Are a Blessing

Today's world is characterized by ambivalence about children. On the one hand, most couples desire to have children, and are upset if their attempts at pregnancy fail. But on the other hand, many couples like to delay having children as long as possible so that their careers and financial stability are established. Even those who long for children often see their arrival as a burden, as a difficult challenge. In the past, it was considered a blessing to have many children. Now many parents like to limit the number of children they have for practical reasons, including financial constraints. As always, we must look to the Scriptures to see what God has to tell us about this topic.

The unambiguous picture we get from the Bible is that children are a blessing. Psalm 127:3–4 says: "Behold, children are a heritage from the LORD, the fruit of the womb a reward. Like arrows in the hand of a warrior are the children of one's youth." The psalm goes on to say that having many children is a sign of blessedness: "Blessed is the man who fills his quiver with them! He shall not be put to shame when he speaks with his enemies in the gate" (v. 5; see also 128:3).

I do not think that there is a strong scriptural case against delaying having children. Sometimes delaying can enable a new couple to concentrate on getting to know and understand each other better during the often-stormy first years of marriage. But we cannot say that the Bible recommends such a delay. Perhaps delaying having children for a long time, because of such factors as not having a good house or the need to progress in one's career, reflects a devaluation of the importance given to children in the Bible. Parenting is a great work, but many today do not consider it to be so. Many think that having children holds back the progress of the parents, especially the mother.

Sometimes parents communicate to their children that they are a burden. A mother might tell her child something like this: "If not for you, I would be in a top position today." Such a statement might slip out of the mother's mouth at an unguarded moment if she resents having to sacrifice her career because of the child. Then a mother might say, "I lost my figure because of you." Often parents tell their children that they are a nuisance to them. Expressions of regret over adopting a child may slip out of parents' mouths if they are having huge problems with that child. Such statements have a damaging effect on children; they can become embedded in their minds and remain as festering wounds. To their simple and immature minds, these words send the message that they are not really wanted by their parents, resulting in the development of deep-seated insecurities.

In the Bible, parenting is presented as a huge responsibility and a noble call from God. Kent and Barbara Hughes' excellent book *The Disciplines of a Godly Family* alerted me to many of the points made in this section. Hughes quotes the nineteenth-century Presbyterian pastor-theologian Robert Dabney, who says, "The education of children for God is the most important business done on earth."[1] There is a great need today to restore the honor of the work of parenting children. This loss of honor is a symptom of a problem that we are finding in the culture and in the church: personal work is not valued highly anymore. People think that there's no time for it in this busy world. So they talk a lot about the need to disciple new believers and to care for young leaders and Christian workers, but no one seems to have the time for it. This attitude has seeped into our ideas about parenthood. Hughes calls this "the deceptive mathematics of worldly thinking that considers pouring out one's life on a hidden few as a scandalous waste of one's potential."[2]

The arrival of a child brings huge changes in the life of a family. There are new financial challenges and new strains on the parents, especially the mother. But we must never fall into the trap of thinking of this as a burden that damages our lives. That attitude will somehow get communicated to our children and do great harm to them. Anything of great value in life is costly. That is how we look at parenting. It is a great privilege, and we dearly love our children and would not exchange them for anything in this world, even though raising them is a strain.

Let Them Know That They Are a Delight to You
Delighting in Children

Looking at our children as a blessing influences our attitude toward them. Paul yearned for his spiritual son Timothy and wrote,

"As I remember your tears, I long to see you, that I may be filled with joy" (2 Tim. 1:4). How important it is for children to know that their parents find them delightful and long to see them. This is the way our heavenly Father looks at us. We often talk about how we should delight in God, which is a very biblical theme. I think, however, that we don't talk enough about how God delights in us. I was able to find six texts that specifically state this (Pss. 35:27; 41:11; 44:3; 147:11; 149:4; Isa 62:4). My favorite verse, Zephaniah 3:17, does not use the word *delight*, but it makes the same point: "The LORD your God is in your midst, a mighty one who will save; he will rejoice over you with gladness; he will quiet you by his love; he will exult over you with loud singing." A respected Hebrew lexicon defines the word translated as "exult" as "shriek ecstatically, shout with joy."[3] The Bible actually teaches that God is thrilled over us!

If that is the way the heavenly Father views his children, we have a model for the way earthly parents should view their children. And because God gave us words as the major way to communicate truth, we must express our delight over our children in words. In chapter 6, I mentioned how praise completes joy in a relationship. So when we praise our children, we increase their joy and ours. There are many instances where Paul expresses delight over his spiritual children, such as these: "Therefore, my brothers, whom I love and long for, my joy and crown, stand firm thus in the Lord, my beloved" (Phil. 4:1) and "For what is our hope or joy or crown of boasting before our Lord Jesus at his coming? Is it not you? For you are our glory and joy" (1 Thess. 2:19–20). Our children should frequently hear such warm words of affirmation from our lips.

Not only do we affirm our children, we also rejoice when they are honored. Paul says, "If one member is honored, all rejoice together" (1 Cor. 12:26). Honoring others is a task to which Christians give themselves with zeal. Paul says, "Outdo one another in showing honor" (Rom. 12:10). We especially need to practice this with our children. We should respond with unmixed joy when they meet with some success or honor. I use the term *unmixed* because sometimes, when someone does well, we might add a qualifying statement after expressing our joy, something like this: "Next time, try to do even better" or "Now don't get too proud, you should give all the glory to God." Sometimes the family can't enjoy a success fully because the parents are preoccupied with boasting about it to others. I think it is a good idea for the family to celebrate an honor in some way. We used to go out for ice cream when our children did well in something. Ice cream was something we could afford only occasionally.

There should be some regular practices in the home that communicate the idea that the parents delight in their children. The first and last things for the day can express affirmation to children. When a child gets up in the morning, the parents should welcome him with joy. When little children go to bed at night, how important it is for parents to be with them, say a prayer, and perhaps tell them a bedtime story. It is a great idea for parents to say goodnight to their adult children also when they go to sleep at night.

When a father comes home after work, he can first express his joy in seeing his wife. Then he can go to his children. He can say something like this to his infant daughter: "Where is my dearest, darling daughter? Oh, there you are!" He could then greet her and give her a big hug. Sometimes children are so happy with this behavior of the father that they run to the door to greet him when he comes home from work. When the children leave the house, however busy the parents are, they should drop everything to acknowledge their children and say something like this: "Bye! Have a good time." All these actions buttress the idea that the children are very dear to their parents. For me, the last example I mentioned can be a challenge. Usually when I am in my office at home, I am busy studying or working on my correspondence. I have to make a clear decision to drop those tasks and concentrate for a moment on my (now adult) child and bid him or her goodbye.

Warren Wiersbe tells of addressing a group of Christian students on the subject of prayer, pointing out that our Father in heaven is always available when we call. To illustrate this, Wiersbe told them that the receptionist at the office of the church where he was pastor had a list of names he had prepared. These people could get through to him at any time, no matter what he was doing. Even if he was in a staff meeting or a counseling session, if any of these people phoned, the receptionist was to call Wiersbe immediately. At the top of this list were the members of his family. Even if a matter might seem to him inconsequential, Wiersbe said, "I want my family to know that I am available." After the service, one of the students said to him: "Would you adopt me? I can never get through to my father, and I need his encouragement so much!"[4]

Sometimes Christians who have not experienced such delight from their parents find it difficult to accept the idea that God is delighted with them. They don't believe that they are delightful people. Not having had a happy model from their parents, they can also find it difficult to express delight over their children. They should be aware of this and make an extra effort to do what may not come naturally to them—to express their delight in their children directly to them. Our children should not suffer because of our weaknesses. We must try to overcome them; as I will show at the end of this chapter, we can do so with God's help.

Desiring to Help

Paul beautifully describes his love for the Thessalonians by comparing it to a mother's attitude toward her children: "But we were gentle among you, like a nursing mother taking care of her own children. So, being affectionately desirous of you, we were ready to share with you not only the gospel of God but also our own selves, because you had become very dear to us" (1 Thess. 2:7–8). Three terms Paul uses well describe a mother's attitude toward her children: she is "gentle," not rough and irritable; she is "affectionately desirous" of them, not distant and difficult to reach; and her children are "very dear" to her, so she does not act unpleasantly with them. These terms all have a sense of affection and longing. To maintain such attitudes, parents need to keep in touch with God and keep receiving the freshness his love brings, as we saw with the story of the lady with the apron in chapter 1.

Armed with these three attitudes, Paul says he does three things that a mother does. A mother does the work of "taking care of her children." The word translated "taking care" has the idea of "to take care of, with the implication of cherishing and concern for."[5] The mother not only takes care of her children, she also cherishes them, that is, she expresses affection to them. Next, she shares the gospel with them. This is the most wonderful thing parents can do for their children—to help secure a wonderful eternity for them. Finally, Paul and his colleagues "were ready to share . . . [their] own selves" with the Thessalonians. Mothers do this so well. But Paul was a spiritual father. This suggests that fathers also should care for their children in these ways. Parents, including fathers, must get close to their children and share their lives with them.

Put briefly, we "make love [our] aim" (1 Cor. 14:1 RSV) in our relationship with our children. Then we do what we can to fulfill that desire, even if it is inconvenient or tiring. The best example of this is the love of a mother, which makes her stay up night after night when a child is sick to care for him. But fathers also must show such love. When our children were young, they would ask me to pick them up after a party or a meeting late at night. Or they would ask whether I could take them to the train station early in the morning—not easy for a night person! Even if I was very tired and wanting to sleep at the time, I would readily do these things. I tried to communicate that these were things I wanted to do; things I was happy to do. And happiness was always my experience when I did these things. Love is costly, but we don't dwell on the cost, because we know it is a beautiful thing we want to do, one for which it is well worth paying the cost. Usually after doing it, we are so happy that we did.

Imagine a father who serves as volunteer leader in his church. His son is running in a key regional track meet and has made it to the finals. The race is at four on Saturday afternoon. But the father also has a meeting of a church committee that he chairs at two o'clock. He explains the situation to his son and tells him that he will try to be there for the finals, but he also says that he might not be able to make it. He calls all the members of the committee on Friday, telling them of his situation and asking them to arrive for the meeting on time. He does the same thing on Saturday morning.

On Saturday, he is able to start the meeting on time and finish it at three-thirty. The father rushes to the stadium where the meet is being held as fast as he can without breaking the speed limit (I say this because once, when on a long trip to see my daughter running, I broke the speed limit and was stopped by a police officer!). He parks his car, runs to the field, and gets there just before the son starts running. As he is running, the son hears his father shouting out, "Go, son!" Spurred by his father's words, he thrusts forward with a burst of speed and wins the race.

The father catches up with his son to congratulate him. The son notices that his father is panting more than him, and he asks him, "I am the one who ran the race; why are you panting?" The father replies, "I needed to be here in time for your race, so I ran." That son is probably not going to be angry about his father's involvement in church. He knows that though his father cares for others in church, he is willing to pay the price of caring for him when necessary.[6] The extra work of calling the committee members on Friday and Saturday, of rushing to the stadium, and of running to the field was part of the cross that came with trying to be obedient to God in all areas. This buttresses what I said in chapter 4, that the balanced life is often our cross. But for the Christian, the cross is always something positive. It's not something we regret.

When We Cannot Be There for Them

Sometimes we cannot do what our children would like us to do for them because of some ministry or other duty. This has been a sad reality in my life and one of the most painful aspects of my traveling ministry. Because my foreign travel schedule fills up about two or three years in advance, I cannot make allowances for important family events that I know about only much later. Not only people in ministry but all busy people have times when they disappoint their children by not being able to be there for important events.

When we know that we are going to be unable to do something or be somewhere that our children would like us to, the worst thing we can do is to snap at them and say something like this: "Don't you realize that I have to do God's work?" Instead, we should express heartfelt sorrow about our inability to do what our children wish us to do.

Paul wanted to visit the Thessalonian church, as they had need of his guidance because of some challenges they faced. He says, "We endeavored the more eagerly and with great desire to see you face to face" (1 Thess. 2:17). But he could not go. So he went through the inconvenience of remaining alone in Athens and sending Timothy to represent him. He says, "Therefore when we could bear it no longer, we were willing to be left behind at Athens alone, and we sent Timothy, our brother and God's coworker in the gospel of Christ, to establish and exhort you in your faith" (3:1–2). Then he adds, "We pray most earnestly night and day that we may see you face to face and supply what is lacking in your faith" (v. 10). He expressed deep sorrow about not being there and did all that could be done to compensate for his absence.

My daughter's graduation from university was a big event in our family. She graduated with high honors, much better than her father did! This was a great joy to me. But I was unable to be at the event because I was in England. As at other universities in Sri Lanka, the date of the graduation ceremonies was announced at the last moment, and I had already planned my trip. In those days, we did not have the means of communication we have now, such as Skype and WhatsApp, but I sent her text messages expressing my sorrow at not being there and my great delight about how well she had done. I still remember the text message that she sent in return. I hope the pain she felt because of my not being there was reduced by my expressions of sorrow.

Yet despite all our efforts, sometimes our family members do not understand the sacrifices we make and are unhappy about things in our ministry. It is too painful for them. We should give our family members the freedom to disagree with us and to express their disagreement without hurting them by being angry about their inability to understand. This is a lonely and painful cross to bear. Jesus had to endure this. Mark records, "The crowd gathered again, so that they could not even eat" (Mark 3:20). This seems to have been the last straw for Jesus's family members. Mark goes on to say, "And when his family heard it, they went out to seize him, for they were saying, 'He is out of his mind'" (v. 21). Many people were blessed by the sacrifices Jesus made, but the people closest to him did not appreciate that. The next verse describes an even more hostile response to Jesus: "And the scribes who came down from Jerusalem were saying, 'He is possessed by Beelzebul,' and 'by the prince of demons he casts out the demons'" (v. 22). Leadership is a tough and costly calling. Despite our hurt, we must act with restraint when we encounter misunderstanding and strenuously avoid causing further harm to our loved ones.

Keeping Promises

Another vitally important aspect of our concern for our children is keeping the promises we make to them. Both Jesus and James said that we do not need to take oaths because a simple yes or no should suffice (Matt. 5:33–37; James 5:12). The damage done by a chain of broken promises by parents is deeper than the disappointment children experience from an individual broken promise. These failures also communicate to the children the idea that the ones they depend on most are not dependable. That could result in severe insecurity, wounding the children in a way that affects them for the rest of their lives. They may find it difficult to trust people and may overreact when people act in an untrustworthy manner. They could even find it difficult to believe that God is reliable. Parents should aspire to be faithful like their heavenly Father, who faithfully keeps all his promises.

Sometimes parents foolishly make promises that are too difficult to keep. But if they make a promise, then they must do all they can to fulfill it, even though that may mean weariness and severe inconvenience. We endure the weariness and inconvenience out of love for our children. This should make us careful about making promises that we cannot fulfill. Sometimes we may be able to fulfill a promise at a later time or in a different way. For instance, an absolutely essential meeting requires that a father call off an outing to the beach with his family, but he gives the next available slot in his schedule to this trip. His children get the message that their father is reliable. He does not forget. He perseveres until he is able to do what he has promised.

Again, when we are forced to break a promise due to unavoidable circumstances, we should focus on the sorrow that the change causes us rather than on the unavoidability of the circumstances. We don't emphasize such statements as: "I can't do it! It's impossible." Rather, we say: "Oh, dear, I wish I could have come. But it's impossible. I'm so sad!" We need to remember that if we keep telling our children that we cannot do things the children like because we are doing God's work, the children could end up resenting God's work. They may see him as their killjoy!

Spending Time with Our Children

There are few things that express love to our children more than spending time with them. This is the way parents impart values to their children. When Jesus chose the twelve apostles as his basic team, it was "so that they might be with him" (Mark 3:14). The other two reasons given have to do with ministry: preaching and casting out demons (vv. 14b–15). Parents sometimes say that they have quality time with their children rather than a large quantity of time. With children, quality requires quantity.

Dorothy and Armour Patterson cite a book, *Women's Quest for Economic Equality*, published in 1988, that claimed that since the 1970s, a child's time with his parents had declined by about ten hours per week.[7] I do not know whether the trend has continued at this rate and what the figures are in my part of the world, but this is evidence of a disturbing pattern that we see all over the world. In more recent times, parents have had to contend with competition from computers and television. We will talk about this in the next chapter. For now, we must say that children spending hours in front of a television or computer may bring some relief to parents, but there is no substitute for personal parental interaction with their children. Computer games and television should never be used as convenient and cheap babysitters![8]

My friend Dr. Lalith Mendis, who was once a medical college lecturer and is now a pastor, has a special interest in developmental issues of children. He tells me that there is a close connection between the time parents spend talking to their children and the healthy development of the children, especially in the area of speech. He says that often the cause for a speech defect is that the mother does not give sufficient time for speech interaction with the child. There are key aspects in person-to-person conversation that are missing in television and digital conversation.[9]

Children learn the security of being loved through long hours spent with their parents, especially their mothers. This is why it is ideal for mothers to give large chunks of time to their children during the first five years of their lives. While grandparents, babysitters, day-care institutions, and preschools can help children, there is no substitute for a mother's attention. Therefore, this should be a major factor that influences the vocational choices young mothers make. Many Christian mothers have chosen to retard their progress in their careers in order to give sufficient time for their children during their earlier years. I had a friend whose wife took several years off from her Christian ministry-related job. Many of her friends felt that she was doing something very wrong. Her now-happy adult children bear testimony to the wisdom of her choice.

Fathers should also spend special times with their children. They can play with them, take them to different places, and watch television with them and discuss what they have seen. I used to find good opportunities to chat with my children when I drove them places. Later, when they began using email and text messaging, I had some serious conversations with them, especially with my son, using those means. Of course, we who are fathers need to get to know the things that our children are interested in if we are to have meaningful conversations with them. If they are interested in music, we need to have some basic understanding of trends in the field. It is the same with sports. We should know about their friends in school and in the neighborhood. These are things that we must make the effort to learn out of commitment to our children.

One of the warmest times of fellowship in a family is when everyone is together at mealtime. Some years ago, I read an article about some research done on the incidence of depression and suicide among teenagers. The researchers found that this problem was markedly less prevalent among teenagers who came from homes where the family members had at least one meal together each day. There is a special warmth of relationship that happens when people eat together. Eating together was a key feature of the fellowship of the earliest church. Luke says, "They broke bread in their homes and ate together with glad and sincere hearts" (Acts 2:46 NIV).

The article also said that when a family eats together, there is an opportunity for each member to sense the feelings of the others. This gives the children a chance to talk about stressful or happy things that they experienced in school. The opportunity to share with loved ones helps to reduce the loneliness and stress levels of teenagers. God has made us to find fulfillment and healing through sharing our joys and sorrows with others. Children can find special help through sharing with their family members because those members have a very significant place in their lives.

This is why I am very uneasy about churches and Christian organizations having too many activities on weekday evenings. Indeed, we must pay a price and come for a few programs. But we must ensure that the family gets together on several evenings each week. Many of the young volunteers in our Youth for Christ ministry come from very dysfunctional homes with no tradition of enjoying meals together. So we try to urge them to change that when they get married. Sometimes pastors who have come from dysfunctional homes do not know the joy and importance of family traditions like this. This is very dangerous, because their churches might present a model of family life that in contrary to the Bible.

A Word to Parents Who Have Not Experienced Delight

Sadly, many parents have not experienced the delight of their own parents. This has left them somewhat handicapped in their ability to express delight over their children. The reality of being deprived of this aspect of love from parents does not change the fact that God loves and delights in his children. The Bible is clear that "to all who did receive him, who believed in his name, he gave the right to become children of God" (John 1:12). The Bible is also clear that God delights in his children, as we saw above. Therefore, all Christians should be able to exclaim the truth of 1 John 3:1–2 with delight. I am quoting a modern paraphrase here, as it captures the emotional tone of these two verses well: "What marvelous love the Father has extended to us! Just look at it—we're called children of God! That's who we really are. But that's also why the world doesn't recognize us or take us seriously, because it has no idea who he is or what he's up to. But friends, that's exactly who we are: children of God" (MESSAGE). All the rejection and neglect we face on earth does not change the fact that God truly loves us as a perfectly loving father would love his own children.

Actually, God's love and care is greater than what any father or mother can give us. He tells his people: "Can a woman forget her nursing child, that she should have no compassion on the son of her womb? Even these may forget, yet I will not forget you" (Isa. 49:15). The love that God's commitment brings to us is well described by Paul when he says, "God's love has been poured into our hearts through the Holy Spirit who has been given to us" (Rom. 5:5). The word translated as "poured" (*ekcheō*) means "to cause someone to experience something in an abundant or full manner."[10] Some translations render it in this verse as "flooded." There is no shortage in God's love. Its abundance can more than compensate for all the deprivation of love and affirmation that one may have had in childhood.

But we must open ourselves to that love. I have seen some who have done so, and it opened the door to the radiance of God's love in their lives. Others prefer to remain angry with life and wallow in self-pity over what they have experienced. The anger of such people will most surely express itself in their relationships with others. Paul teaches that letting the sun go down on our anger and giving the Devil a foothold are connected (Eph. 4:26–27). Those who remain angry eventually become Satan's agents in hurting others, including their children. If this is so, one of the most important tasks facing people who were deprived of love and affirmation is that of opening themselves to God's love. They may need to be guided by another person, such as a counselor, a friend, or a pastor, in this process of finding release from anger and openness to God's love. But they must do whatever it takes so that they will not hurt themselves and their children.

Conclusion

The challenges of parenting are immense. As parents struggle, especially in the early years of a child's life, their burdens may be so heavy that they can forget what a great work parenting is. They should try to remember that the Bible views parenting as a noble calling. After all, most great victories are won by paying a big price. Indeed, parents pay a huge price to raise up healthy children. Even though society may not regard parenting as prestigious work, it is a high and rewarding call in God's sight. May that biblical perspective help sustain parents when they have to endure the pains and strains of parenting.

11

Fun, Traditions, and Security for Children

In the previous chapter, we started looking at the home environment Christian parents should foster in order to nurture healthy, happy, and holy children. We said that the delight of the parents over their children is an important ingredient in a Christian home. Now we will look at three ways in which this delight over children is worked out: fun, traditions, and security.

Children and Youth Like to Have Fun

Fun-Friendly Families

When Christian parents think of the welfare of their children, they usually think of protecting them from harmful influences and motivating them to develop habits that will help them to progress in life. So they give considerable attention to moral instruction and education. However, there are other vital aspects of healthy growth that they should not ignore. One of these is the need for children and youth to enjoy healthy fun during their growing-up years.

Talking about the coming peace and prosperity of Jerusalem, Zechariah says, "And the streets of the city shall be full of boys and girls playing in its streets" (Zech. 8:5). Jesus used a picture of children playing in the streets for one of his parables. The game was probably a mock wedding, which included dancing in response to the playing of a flute (Matt. 11:16–17). While there are no references to toys in the Old Testament, archaeologists have found "whistles, rattles, marbles, dolls, animals (at times with wheels), and other objects on numerous sites in Palestine [which] give some indication of the types of toys with which the Israelite young played."[1] We can safely say that fun was an important feature of the life of children in biblical times.

I often tell parents of little children that it may be more important for their children to play in their early years than to study. They can start studying when they start going to school. It is important that their childhoods be filled with pleasant memories, including those of playing with family members and others. Parents should look for places with amusements for children and take them there frequently. And they should carve out times in their schedules to play with their children. We may not feel like doing so, but it can be a great blessing to both the children and to us. I have already mentioned how, when my young son would ask me to play cricket with him, I often did not feel an inclination to do so. But out of a sense of duty, I went to play, and I always came back refreshed and glad that I had gone.

We should make our homes "fun-friendly" places. Sometimes we are so eager to keep our homes looking spick-and-span that we restrict the fun our children can have at home. That is not healthy. I know of families that have designated one wall in the house where the little children can scribble and draw. Our son loved to play cricket. But the place in our yard where he could play was near to some windows, which the ball could easily hit and break. One of our creative Youth for Christ staff members made a cover for the windows with a wooden frame and wire mesh. That arrangement was not beautiful, but it protected the windows and gave my son freedom to play without fear. Allowing children to play without fear is a key. If they have positive attitudes to play, then they will be more open to our wishes that they stop at certain times so as to come home and do homework. The freedom to play will not be something they have to fight to safeguard.

Ecclesiastes recognizes the inclination of youth to have fun and encourages them to give expression to it: "Rejoice, O young man, in your youth, and let your heart cheer you in the days of your youth. Walk in the ways of your heart and the sight of your eyes" (Eccl. 11:9a). Of course, it goes on to say, "But know that for all these things God will bring you into judgment" (v. 9b), showing that we must have fun in keeping with God's principles—holy fun. Happiness is never the primary goal for our children; holiness is. Children must learn how to have responsible fun; fun that does not hurt or inconvenience others. The ideal place to learn that is the home. We have faced a problem relating to fun in our Youth for Christ ministry among unreached youth. We believe very much in giving the youth an opportunity to have clean fun. But often they go to an extreme and the fun becomes unholy. I think a major reason for this is that they have not learned the discipline of having clean and responsible fun at home.

We often quote the statement given two verses later: "Remember also your Creator in the days of your youth" (Eccl. 12:1a). But we forget the reason given for remembering one's Creator when young: ". . . before the evil days come and the years draw near of which you will say, 'I have no pleasure in them'" (v. 1b). The verses that follow show that the rationale for this appeal is that old people, with their aching backs and creaking bones, cannot enjoy life as young people do. Therefore, youth are told to remember their Creator at the age when they can enjoy themselves—for in companionship with the Creator of our capacity for fun, we can have the best and most enjoyable kind of fun.

When children and youth grow up enjoying clean and healthy fun at home, they will not be as vulnerable to the lure of sinful fun that will soon hit them with great force. The world thinks that to have fun, one must sin! I once saw a birthday card that said: "It's your birthday. Enjoy yourself. Sin a little." We need to demonstrate to our children that fun is compatible with Christianity, and that the only way to have really enjoyable fun is to do it along with God. Allowing them to enjoy fun times with their earthly parents is a good way to open their minds to the idea that they can enjoy spending time with their heavenly Father too.

The Commercialization and Competitiveness of Fun

It seems that almost everything in life is becoming commercialized and subject to fierce competition, and, sadly, sports and many fun activities of children and youth have also gone that way. Sports do not function as a source of enjoyment to many who play today. Actually, sports can become an idol in a child's life. A child who is clearly talented in a sport should be encouraged to pursue it, but we should be careful about pushing our children too hard here. Sometimes parents want their children to achieve the things that they could not achieve in their youth, so they apply unhealthy pressure on their children to perform. Only eleven starters and a few substitutes can make a soccer team. That means most children are going to miss out. Parents should remember this and not put undue pressure on their children. They could end up causing their children to be deprived of joyful character.

Sometimes sports practices, band and choir practices, and other events take place on Sundays during Sunday school or worship times. In these cases, children may miss being at church for a whole season. In Sri Lanka, some children don't come to church because they have to go to extra tutorial classes during church times. As Chip Ingram puts it, "That's a great way to teach your children that being a star is more important than being a worshipper."[2] Parents must always remember the words of Jesus: "For what does it profit a man to gain the whole world and forfeit his soul? For what can a man give in return for his soul?" (Mark 8:36–37).

Television and the Cyber World

We need to say a word about children's cartoons and other programs on television that often provide parents with release from the strains of caring for little ones. Watching a few carefully chosen cartoons and other programs, such as documentaries; science, nature, and sports programs; and good movies and short films may be healthy for children. But studies show that indiscriminate watching can harm them. Watching violence on TV can make children less sensitive to pain and suffering. The speed of the images is said to damage the brain and eyes. The passivity of children while watching is said to impede proper speech development.[3] So parents must do their homework to ensure that what their children watch is not harmful to them.[4]

The same could be said about iPads, tablet PCs, smartphones, and video games, all of which influence many older children much more than television. Many informed parents are now withholding these devices until their children are past their childhood years because of possible negative effects on healthy growth in important areas. A lot of what I know about this area I have learned from my children. Their generation knows much more than mine, especially about the cyber world. It could be a great joy for our children to see the roles reversed as they teach us about how the cyber world and gadgets such as smartphones work!

One of the most serious adverse effects of such things as TV, smartphones, and computers on children is that they can rob them of healthy physical activity, of time spent playing games and sports outdoors. The time that an earlier generation of children spent outdoors, the current generation spends indoors at the computer, on a smartphone, or in front of a television set. By retreating into the private world of computers, television, and video games, many children also miss the benefits of playing team games, with all the character development that takes place through them. Setting carefully thought-out rules for all of these activities aids the healthy development of children.

Parents should know what happens when their children are on the Internet. Private chats on social media, especially with applications such as Snapchat, can be very harmful. Young people can view and chat with nude women on live webcams for free—it is only a click away![5] Like many other things relating to the information-technology revolution, social media can be used for good and bad purposes. In Sri Lanka, several girls have committed suicide as a result of character assassination on Facebook, mainly the posting of photos of them in compromising situations by angry ex-boyfriends. Parents need to know about activities that can have such a powerful influence on their children.

Parents also should be aware of the ready access to pornography. Parents should be able to monitor their children's activities on computers and phones in some way. This is easier said than done. They need to impose restrictions, set up filters, and bring in accountability systems to ensure their children don't ruin their lives. The price is well worth paying to protect our children (and adults). Children should be warned about looking at polluting things on their mobile phones. Sadly, many young people ruin their marriages before they begin by watching things that pollute their minds. Pornography and computer games are extremely addictive, and therefore parents should very seriously consider how they can help protect their children from harm. They must not stay uninvolved, saying that they don't know about these things, while their children ruin their lives.

Satan has found ways of spoiling every good thing on earth. That is what he has done with fun. May God redeem fun in our lives and those of our children so that we can have the best kind of fun: holy fun!

Traditions and Celebrations

One of the ways the atmosphere of joy is preserved in the home is through happy family traditions and celebrations. I have an uncle who is a pediatrician. When our first child was an infant, he told me something that had a marked influence on the way we reared our children. He said children need regularity. Without regular routines, they become insecure. This was an important point to me, as my calling makes my schedule somewhat irregular. Just as children like the world around them to feel secure, they also find special fulfillment in regular practices devoted to enjoyment that become traditions in the home. Tim Stafford says, "It's in our makeup as human beings to set aside certain times and days to celebrate."[6] We need to make such opportunities possible in our families.

God made provision for this in the Old Testament by instituting festivals or feasts. There were private feasts, which usually celebrated an important time in a family, such as a wedding (Gen. 29:22ff.); the weaning of a child (Gen. 21:8); the visit of a guest (Gen. 19:3); or the beginning of harvest (Ex. 23:16). The birthdays of Pharaoh and King Herod are mentioned as feast occasions (Gen. 40:20; Mark 6:21), but not birthdays of the covenant people of God. Job 1:4 says that Job's "sons used to go and hold a feast in the house of each one on his day." Those days may have been their birthdays. I believe the idea of a birthday party fits in with the biblical idea of celebrating with others in special times of thanksgiving to God.

The communal feasts were the weekly Sabbath, the monthly new moon festival, and the three annual feasts: Passover, Pentecost, and Tabernacles. These feasts placed a heavy emphasis both on family activities and on celebrating God's provision. So the Bible instructed families to eat their festival meals with rejoicing (Deut. 16:11, 14–15; 2 Chron. 30:21). These were very lavish occasions. "Although meat was relatively scarce in Hebrew society, it was conspicuously present at several of the festivals, where the requirement of animal sacrifices insured a large-scale banquet of meat."[7] The popular *Dictionary of Biblical Imagery* says, "A holiday spirit also pervaded Old Testament festivals," and cites the following description of the feast of Purim: "Therefore the

Jews . . . hold the fourteenth day of the month of Adar as a day for gladness and feasting, as a holiday, and as a day on which they send gifts of food to one another" (Est. 9:19). The article goes on to say that festivals "were accompanied by high-spiritedness and a letting go of usual inhibitions."[8]

The times of communal celebrations were also marked by musical expressions of joy and thanksgiving, as the following description indicates:

> Sing aloud to God our strength;
> shout for joy to the God of Jacob!
> Raise a song; sound the tambourine,
> the sweet lyre with the harp.
> Blow the trumpet at the new moon,
> at the full moon, on our feast day.
> For it is a statute for Israel,
> a rule of the God of Jacob. (Ps. 81:1–4)

God decreed that the people should rejoice with music on the feast day.

It is not an accident that music has become a major factor in the celebration of the two main Christian festivals, Easter and Christmas. John Wesley said, "Singing is as much the language of holy joy, as praying is of holy desire."[9] Sometimes the performance orientation of our Christmas and Easter programs can take away the joy of them, but that does not need to be the case. One can be committed to high quality without sacrificing enjoyment. The great composer Joseph Haydn (1732–1809) was once asked why his church music was so cheerful. He replied: "When I think upon God, my heart is so full of joy that the notes dance and leap, as it were, from my pen, and since God has given me a cheerful heart it will be pardoned me that I serve Him with a cheerful spirit."[10]

Children need to know that they can look forward to fun times during festivals. But Stafford points out a major challenge that leaders face when it comes to celebrations: "Celebrations take time. Busy people don't always take the time required. Even if it's a national holiday . . . they want to accomplish so much that they don't relax and celebrate. They just don't see the point." This comes from an orientation that does not view tradition and celebration as God-given gifts to us. Stafford continues: "Holidays don't have a utilitarian purpose. There is no lesson to be learned from watching a parade. Which is part of the point. The point is there is no point. Joy is not about accomplishing something."[11]

When our children were with us, we developed some traditions that became meaningful aspects of our Christmas celebrations. We set apart one day in December for shopping. As Christmas is a busy time for me, I entered the shopping day in my datebook several weeks before Christmas Day. When my daughter was old enough, she began to plan out the day: where we would go to shop, where we would eat, and so on. We usually decorated the house on Christmas Eve. This, too, was done as a family.

The Jews viewed the Sabbath day also as a festival. They had special traditions for the keeping of this day, which was a very family-oriented day. Today we should try to ensure that we have a Sabbath rest so the family can refresh itself. For those of us in ministry, Sunday is not a day of rest. I used to take Wednesday off each week (now, while I ensure that I take one day off each week, it is not necessarily the same day each week). If my children heard me involved in a conversation that suggested I was not going to be free on Wednesday, they would interject by saying something like this: "But that's your off day!" They looked forward to the fact that the family had my undivided attention on that day.

Vacations are another important tradition for a family. Ask an adult about pleasant memories of happy experiences he or she had as a child, and invariably family vacations will be mentioned. Today, many Christian leaders cannot afford to go to traditional vacation sites. Therefore, they must use their creativity to find places that will give the family the joy of spending holidays together. I know of people who visit friends and relatives in other towns. When my children were small, we once went to a place by the beach for our vacation. As we got out of the car, my daughter said, "I hope there are no Christians here!" She knew that if there were Christians, I would be distracted by people who wanted to talk to me. As we walked into the resort, there right in front was a group from a church where I often had spoken! They had come on a church retreat. The leaders must have instructed the people to leave us alone, because no one came and spoke to us! This incident showed me how much our children want us to give them our full attention during fun times.

There are other celebrations that I can think of, such as birthdays and anniversaries. Here again, we should think of enjoying such times not for show but for the joy of the family. For our birthdays, my wife and I often decided that we would just celebrate as a family without inviting others. It is part of my job to be at the celebrations of many people. We thought that one way we could compensate for that public lifestyle was to have our birthdays in private. The children, of course, liked to enjoy their birthdays with their friends. But we need to remember the important principle of true joy over mere appearance. Some people in Sri Lanka like to put on a big show for a child's first birthday—a day the child will not remember. If it is a big party, it can become a confusing and frightening experience for the child. I know of people who have gone into debt in order to have such parties. Such celebrations do not contribute to the joy of the family, especially if they leave the family saddled with a debt.

Nurturing Secure Children
We live in a world where insecurity has reached epidemic proportions. Extremism and the rage of angry psychotics have left us all vulnerable to the possibility of being victims of violent attacks. Our culture pushes us to look at others as competitors, with the result that we see people who should be our friends as threats to us. Our commitment to comfort and ease can drive us to blame

other people, especially children, for reducing our comfort or convenience. The presence of predators, especially those who target young people, can make this world an insecure place for children.

How can we counter these trends? One way in which people can grow into secure individuals is by experiencing the warmth of love and care in their families. When people grow up loved, they are less vulnerable to the temptation to go unhealthy ways in search of security in their lives.

A Mother's Love Protects the Children

In the previous chapter, we saw that Paul describes his ministry in Thessalonica as similar to the behavior of a mother. Paul says, "So, being affectionately desirous of you, we were ready to share with you not only the gospel of God but also our own selves, because you had become very dear to us" (1 Thess. 2:8). "Affectionately desirous" translates a Greek word (*homeiromai*) that carries the idea of experiencing a yearning affection for someone.[12] As we said in the last chapter, children should know that their mothers yearn for them. They are not mistakes or nuisances. Paul is saying that a mother longs to see her children and is "delighted" (NIV) to share her life with them. When she looks after her children at great personal cost, she does not do it reluctantly, only out of a sense of duty, but willingly, out of an attitude of delight. The Greek word translated as "ready" in the ESV is a strong word justifying the NIV translation "delighted."

We looked at the value of the delight of parents over their children in the last chapter. Here I want to discuss some other benefits of such care. From the time they are very young, children face rejection and hurt from a hostile culture. It is amazing how much hurt can be inflicted by classmates in school even during preadolescent years. In a competitive world, where children constantly face rejection and are made to feel inferior to others, how refreshing it is for them to know that their mothers are delighted over them and are happy to do whatever is necessary for their welfare. It gives them a sense of self-worth. The mother's affectionate desiring and delighted self-giving (1 Thess. 2:8) help overcome the rejection children experience.

In the same section in 1 Thessalonians, Paul says, "But we were gentle among you, like a nursing mother taking care of her own children" (v. 7). As I noted in the previous chapter, the word translated as "taking care" carries the ideas of cherishing and concern. Leon Morris says, "The verb *caring* means basically 'to warm'; it is used of the mother bird (Deut. 22:6), and so comes to have the secondary meaning, 'to cherish,' 'to care for tenderly.'"[13] The fact that this is done gently suggests that the mother is sensitive to the child's unique needs and personality.

I think children are more vulnerable to bad influences today than ever before in history. Sexual abuse of children is rampant in the world today; children can be exposed to ever-accessible pornography and violence through the media or the Internet; and one can never be sure whether children are protected from bad influences in their neighborhoods and schools. Vigilance by mothers (and fathers) goes a long way toward combatting these bad influences. This vigilance is motivated by the affectionate desire, the delighted self-giving, and the gentle caring of a mother, as Paul describes. The result of such motherly love is security. Desire for and delight in our children gives them self-worth in a competitive culture that often excludes people. Gentle care gives a child protection from dangerous influences.

Incomplete Attention Can Harm Children

I sometimes take pride at my ability to multitask, though that ability is gradually diminishing with age. Yet multitasking can cause problems in a relationship. My wife gets quite annoyed when I am working at my computer or on my phone while she is talking to me. I claim that I can carry on a good conversation while I am doing these things, but I know I am not giving her my full attention.

This kind of incomplete attention can be very damaging to little children. If their mothers are always working with their mobile phones while they are caring for their children, the children miss the richness that comes from a mother's undivided attention. Considering how serious a problem busyness is for parents today, they should be very careful about adding things that prevent them from giving their full attention to their children and to each other.

Having hundreds of friends on Facebook can leave us with less time to nurture deep and intimate relationships with those who are closest to us. Proverbs 18:24 may have something significant to tell our digital generation, with its addiction to social media: "A man of many companions may come to ruin, but there is a friend who sticks closer than a brother." By having too many friends with whom we can have only superficial relationships, we can ruin our relationships with those who are most important to us, such as our spouses, children, and close friends.

I have been intimately associated with the Christian drug rehab community in Sri Lanka for the past twenty years or so. One of the first observations I made was that the mothers of a majority of the students in the Youth for Christ drug rehab center had worked abroad, away from their families, for many years when these students were growing up. Subsequently, I found out that this was a nationwide reality. To help the family get out of grinding poverty, the mother leaves home and works very hard. With the wife away, the husband often turns to alcohol and sometimes has an affair with another woman. The children are not properly cared for. The grandparents or relatives looking after them do not have the knowledge or the ability to protect them from such things as abuse and the Internet. The result is that many of these children, especially girls, are sexually abused. The boys get addicted to pornography. These problems can ruin their chances of happy sexual relationships in marriage. More immediately, they often find that drugs temporarily fill the aching void in their hearts created by the absence of their mothers.

Mothers who go to work outside their homes should bear these dangers in mind and ask whether they are going to miss providing their children the opportunity to grow up in a secure environment. They may choose to take a job that does not pay what they are qualified to earn in order to be with their children for more time. Or they may decide to stay at home for a few years when the children are little. Doing so may hamper their prospects of professional advancement, but this is a price worth paying in order to nurture secure children.

Children who have been subjected to abuse enter adulthood with severe handicaps. Children who have been unfairly subjected to severe punishments may have abnormally high levels of rage in adulthood when they see unfair treatment. In his book *Healing for Damaged Emotions*, David Seamands points out that "whenever you experience a response on your part that is way out of proportion to the stimulus, then look out. You have probably tapped into some deeply hidden emotional hurt."[14] Sometimes people develop a huge struggle with lust as a result of sexual abuse in their younger years. No one knows about it until there is a sudden prominent moral lapse, then everyone is shocked. But sexual abuse can result in the opposite response—a great distaste for sex, which also can adversely affect marriages.

Thankfully, sensitive counseling can bring healing through God's grace to such wounds. We need to talk about these issues in Christian circles so that wounded people can pluck up the courage to seek help. But how much better it would have been if they had been protected from these experiences!

Protecting children is one of the major tasks of parents—a task that is getting harder and harder today. The Bible is loaded with warnings to God's people against harmful influences. There are two verbs in the Gospels that carry the idea of warning of danger. One (*prosechō*) is translated "beware" or "be on guard"; it appears ten times. The other (*blepō*) usually means "see"; it appears ten times in the Gospels with the sense of "be alert," "watch out," or "be on guard." So there are twenty places in the teaching of Jesus that carry the idea of warnings about danger. Paul often warned the readers of his epistles of doctrinal and moral dangers. Similarly, parents must warn their children of the dangers in the world. I am very grateful to my mother, who, when I was in my youth, constantly warned me about the dangers of the false values of modern culture. I think it gave me a healthy disdain for world-liness, which, in turn, acted as a deterrent to being carried away with some harmful worldly trends. So parents must try to ensure that their children are not overcome by influences that can harm their growth.

Parents' Love Combats Comparison

Our children face great handicaps as a result of growing up in a culture where people are compared and contrasted with others and where others progress by cutting them down. In Sri Lanka, according to the warped, worldly sense of values of some people, fair-skinned girls are regarded as more beautiful than dark-skinned girls. I have heard Christians—who, I believe, do not intend to be unkind—say very unkind things to children, such as, "Why are you so dark?" or "She is so much fairer than you." Other such statements include "Why are you so short?" or "Couldn't you lose some weight?" Children who face this kind of rejection because of a supposed handicap they have can grow up with the insecurity of thinking that they are not desirable to those of the other sex because they are "ugly." When they become young people, they may be vulnerable to relationships that are harmful to them.

We have seen this happening in our ministry. A girl comes to Christ and finds great refuge from a hostile world in the warmth of Christian fellowship. She is ready to be used in the service of God. But wounds remain from the constant words of rejection she faced at home or at school. Then she finds a young man who shows her attention and affirms her as no one has done before. She cannot resist the lure of this affirmation. She develops a relationship with him and may move in with this person who seems to love her so much. But within a few days, she realizes that she has made a huge mistake because the young man is now treating her abusively. Because of a thirst for affirmation, a person who has lacked it can fall into the trap of developing a romantic relationship with the first person who provides it—a person who happens to be totally unsuited for him or her.

Often parents are guilty of wounding their children through insensitive words. Sometimes parents compare them with others in order to motivate them to do good. Parents who experienced such comparison in their youth may resort to comparing their own children with others in the same way. This is a learned behavior that needs to be unlearned. Sadly, unlearning it is not easy. It can be so much a part of a parent's nature that he or she resorts to it naturally. When a child comes home with her report card at the end of the year, her mother might look it over, then ask about cousin Mary's ranking in class. Immediately the girl realizes that her value is being judged by how well her cousin did.

This is only one of many problems that children encounter in a world where their value is judged by such things as beauty, brains, talent, wealth, and family background. The Bible teaches the inestimable value of each and every person in the world. But the world keeps attacking that idea. Parents who affirm their children and communicate to them a strong message about their value can help to heal the wounds children receive from the comparison and rejection in the world around them. A child who has been affirmed and not been subjected to comparison at home will grow up to be a secure adult. If a child gets the sense that she is accepted as a beautiful person at home, declarations about her lack of beauty by an unsuitable person will not have power over her. But a child who is always compared with others and rarely affirmed may grow up to be an unhappy adult.

When parents compare siblings, the siblings grow up with wounds relating to their own brother or sister. These wounds can surface in adult life, when siblings find themselves fighting with each other. The parents watch in dismay as the children battle it out over the family wealth or perhaps even over the care of the parents. The worst consequences come when parents favor one child over another. Here the wounds are even deeper and the disharmony can be even more marked. The story of Jacob's sons bears testimony to the folly of favoring one child over others.

The answer is for parents to love their children equally and not have the same expectations for all the children. One child may be good with technical things, while another may be good at academics. Each has his or her unique gifting, and parents need to look for those gifts and encourage them. Of course, exemplary people can be held up as examples to follow. But this should be done in a way that motivates rather than devalues the child. With all the rejection that people face in this hostile world, the home should be a place of affirmation and acceptance.

Conclusion

This has been a somewhat frightening chapter! We have discussed some of the dangerous influences children face today. But as the saying goes, forewarned is forearmed. Awareness of the challenges that confront our children helps us to equip them to face these challenges wisely. We need to approach parenting with a strong commitment to learn whatever we need to learn for the benefit of our children. We want the best for them, so we must pay the price to learn how to give them the best possible opportunities to grow into healthy, happy, and holy children.

12

Disciplining Children

In the previous two chapters, we talked about such topics as delight and fun. But we cannot stop there. Children need to be delighted in and given opportunities for fun. However, they are born depraved, which means they make mistakes and can be enticed into doing wrong. So they need discipline.

The Bible often talks about how God disciplines us. It often uses the illustration of a father disciplining his children. Moses says, "Know then in your heart that, as a man disciplines his son, the LORD your God disciplines you" (Deut. 8:5). Disciplining children is one of the most important responsibilities of parents.

Introduce Them to God's Holiness

The basis of disciplining in the Christian life is the nature of God. Because God is holy, he hates our sin. Habakkuk 1:13 says that God is "of purer eyes than to see evil and cannot look at wrong." The history of ancient Israel was a story of disobedience followed by discipline, which was followed by repentance as a consequence of the discipline. Therefore, the people of Israel often were told to remember how God had disciplined them. In Deuteronomy 11:1 and 8, there are exhortations to the Israelites to obey the law. Between these two verses is a recounting of how God delivered them mightily (vv. 2–4) and how he punished them severely for their sin (vv. 5–7). That is the pattern of Old Testament history. God wishes to bless his people, but he must punish them for their sin so that they will learn to be holy. A little later, Moses says, "See, I am setting before you today a blessing and a curse: the blessing, if you obey the commandments of the LORD your God, which I command you today, and the curse, if you do not obey the commandments of the LORD your God" (Deut. 11:26–28).

After referring to some stories of judgment in the Old Testament, Paul says, "These things happened to them as examples and were written down as warnings for us" (1 Cor. 10:11 NIV). If that is a purpose for the recording of Old Testament stories of judgment and deliverance, we must tell those stories to our children. Then they will get into their minds the truth that sin is serious in the sight of God. Paul tells the Roman Christians: "Note then the kindness and the severity of God: severity toward those who have fallen, but God's kindness to you, provided you continue in his kindness. Otherwise you too will be cut off" (Rom. 11:22).

Our children need to grow up thinking of God in this way, and for that to happen, they need a good diet of Old Testament history. Our failure to provide this will result in our children growing up with a tolerant attitude toward sin: an attitude they pick up from the culture in which they live. They will find it difficult to understand why their parents' generation gets so agitated over such things as same-sex marriage and abortion, to the point of refusing to allow them to be practiced within Christian circles. They live in a culture where approval of homosexual marriage and abortion is growing, where both are considered basic human rights. Such attitudes were common in biblical times, too, especially in the city of Corinth. So when Paul found gross sexual sin there, he said that the sinner should be disciplined (1 Cor. 5:5). Our children may see this as a gross violation of a human right. They need to be exposed to conscientious teaching of the Bible, both the pleasant passages that talk of blessings and the difficult passages that describe judgment. Our failure to tell these stories to our children will make it difficult for them to have a biblical attitude toward discipline by their parents.

Heed Paul's Advice

Paul has some important teaching for fathers about disciplining children, teaching that deserves our serious consideration. Ephesians 6:4 is a good base to use for this study. There Paul says, "Fathers, do not provoke your children to anger, but bring them up in the discipline and instruction of the Lord." I want to look at each affirmation in this verse.

Do Not Provoke

First, Paul tells fathers not to "provoke" their children. Within the context of disciplining, such provocation would include unreasonable, unjust, uncontrolled, or insulting discipline. Parents often discipline their children out of personal annoyance. I suppose this is inevitable. It is quite natural for parents to get annoyed when their children do wrong. But they can go to extremes, so that the primary message the child gets is "Father is angry" rather than "I did something wrong, but this discipline is for my good, so that I will change."

In Colossians 3:21, part of a parallel passage to Ephesians 6:1–9, Paul says, "Fathers, do not provoke your children, lest they become discouraged." Discipline should encourage children. When Paul talked about what to do with people who were causing trouble in the church, he used some strong language to the somewhat timid Timothy: "This charge I entrust to you, Timothy, my child, in accordance with the prophecies previously made about you, that by them you may wage the good warfare" (1 Tim. 1:18). In the original, the word translated as "charge" is a military term; it is translated as "command" in the NIV. But Paul says that the background for the charge he makes is "the prophecies previously made about you." These prophecies seem to have been the basis of Paul's ambitions for Timothy, and the command was one step in helping him achieve those ambitions. Discipline should encourage children to aspire to greatness rather than discourage them into thinking they are worthless people.

Here are some statements that discourage children: "You are an idiot!" "You are useless!" "You bring shame on our family!" "Why can't you be like your brother?" or "You are such a nuisance!" But statements that do not discourage are more like these: "How could you do such an awful thing? This is not how God wishes you to be!" "Don't you realize how much this is hurting you?" "I will have to punish you, because I want to see you come out of this mess" or "God made you to be a great person, and he will help you through this."

A teenager once told the well-known American preacher Warren Wiersbe, "My father would use a cannon to kill a mosquito!"[1] How many children have been deeply hurt by a parent's unjust and wounding outbursts? I have had a few "rituals of healing" with some adults who were hurt by their parents (usually the fathers). In the presence of God and using Scripture, we go through the painful memories and seek to apply the truths of God's Word to them. The hope is that the person will forgive his or her parents and accept that God is going to turn this painful experience into something good.

All of this suggests that we need the help of God when we discipline. When Paul was in Cyprus, the Roman governor showed a keen interest in the gospel. But a Jewish magician named Elymas tried to prevent him from receiving the message. Paul rebuked him so that he went blind for a while. The report of the harsh words spoken by Paul is preceded by the observation that Paul was "filled with the Holy Spirit" when he spoke (Acts 13:9). We also need the fullness of the Spirit when we must rebuke! So while we rebuke a child, we should be secretly praying hard, pleading for God's help. Unfortunately, when we are angry with a child for doing something wrong, we can act as if we have taken leave from God for a short while so as to do what we need to do.

In this regard, I must mention a sad scenario that I have seen all too often. The mother must slave to give some sense of security to a family that has been ravaged by her husband's irresponsible behavior. Owing to drugs, alcohol, extramarital affairs, or just callousness, the husband does not supply the funds needed to run the home, and when he is at home, he is angry and does hurtful things, especially to his wife. The wife has to work hard to help keep the family afloat economically. Being under so much pressure, she gets annoyed by things the children do and often reacts excessively. The result is that the children are hurt by the very person who is sacrificing her life for them. In this all-too-common scenario, the church needs to do all it can to minister to this terribly harassed family—spiritually, emotionally, physically, legally, and economically. The mother's reactions are not acceptable, but her situation is desperate, necessitating intervention by God's people.

What I have said above does not mean that we do not get angry when our children do wrong things. Wrath is a part of God's personality. He loves us so much that he is angered by the wrong we do. And as God's people, we too must get angry when our loved ones do wrong things. But as Paul says, we get "angry and [we] do not sin" (Eph. 4:26). That is why it is so important to affirm God's presence when we are disciplining. You cannot say hurtful and obscene things when you are aware that God is around! Amid the anger, you realize that God is with you. That gives you the security of being enveloped by the almighty God. This security acts as a preventative against expressing your anger in harmful ways.

Discipline Lovingly

However, we can go overboard in our sensitivity to the harmful effects of harsh discipline. James Dobson says: "Much has been written about the dangers of harsh, oppressive, unloving discipline; these warnings are valid and should be heeded. However, the consequences of oppressive discipline have been cited as justification for the abdication of leadership. That is foolish."[2] Paul's next affirmation in Ephesians 6:4 provides a needed corrective to this danger. After saying, "Fathers, do not provoke your children to anger," he adds, "but bring them up in the discipline . . . of the Lord."

Children need to be disciplined. The word translated as "discipline," *paideia*, carries the idea "to train someone in accordance with proper rules of conduct and behavior."[3] From this Greek word, we get the English term *pedagogy*, which is the art of teaching. When a parent disciplines a child, the focus is more on training than on punishing.

The Bible presents the discipline of a father as an illustration of God's discipline of his children. Hebrews 12:7 says: "It is for discipline that you have to endure. God is treating you as sons. For what son is there whom his father does not discipline?" In the Old Testament, Eli is presented as having failed as a father for not disciplining his sons. God tells the young Samuel about Eli, "I have warned him that judgment is coming upon his family forever, because his sons are blaspheming God and he hasn't disciplined them" (1 Sam. 3:13 NLT). Proverbs says, "Whoever spares the rod hates his son, but he who loves him is diligent to discipline him" (13:24) and "Do not withhold discipline from a child; if you strike him with a rod, he will not die" (23:13). Striking children is outlawed in many countries because it sometimes has caused permanent harm to children. But the teaching of the Bible that children must be disciplined still remains urgently important everywhere.

We must not forget that discipline is actually an expression of love, and that fact must shine through in our discipline. Proverbs says, "The LORD reproves him whom he loves, as a father the son in whom he delights" (3:12). Children should get the impression that parents discipline them because of love for them and that their overall attitude to the child is one of delight.

Dobson has shown that disciplining properly is an act that buttresses the self-worth of a child. If parents simply ignore the wrongs committed by a child, they send the message that the child's actions are not significant enough to merit a reaction. Such children could end up as delinquents—doing spectacular acts of wrong to win the attention of people.[4] Proper discipline helps a child to discover his true identity as a valued member of the family, one whose actions are taken very seriously. Hebrews says: "If you are left without discipline, in which all have participated, then you are illegitimate children and not sons" (12:8). The failure to discipline is a sign that the child is not treated as a true member of the family.

In the previous section, I pointed to scriptural teaching on the dangers of uncontrolled discipline. In this section, I have simply highlighted the strong evidence that disciplining children is an important responsibility within the biblical approach to family life. Parents should think about it seriously and develop their own style of being biblical. Personalities differ; most times, the father and the mother have different styles of disciplining. That is all right, so long as there is no disagreement about the discipline in front of the children—as we shall see below.

Instruct Knowledgeably

The next advice by Paul to fathers in Ephesians 6:4 is to instruct the children. He says, "Bring them up in the . . . instruction of the Lord." The word translated as "instruction" is *nouthesia*, which carries the idea "to provide instruction so as to correct behavior and belief."[5] Disciplining gives parents an opportunity to instruct children. We need to tell them why a certain action is wrong. We need to demonstrate to them why the Christian way of doing something is the best way.

As children today live in a very different world than that in which their parents grew up, parents need to find out about this world. They have to do their homework, and sometimes the best way to do this is to ask their children about it. Taking pains to find out about the world of their children is an aspect of their commitment to their children.

We must be prepared for them to disagree with us and to want to dialogue with us over the truth we are contending for. Once we know the way our children are thinking, we may have to do some serious study in order to respond intelligently to their questions and objections. If we lay down the law without listening to their objections, we will lose the battle for their minds. Instructing children is an aspect of our call to "contend for the faith that was once for all delivered to the saints" (Jude 3). Apologetics is a key aspect of parenting. We approach our children like cross-cultural missionaries. We are patient and eager to learn and identify with them so that, from within their thought world, we can influence them toward God's thoughts. We will talk more about this in the next chapter.

Our aim in our teaching is to give our children a Christian understanding of the issue they are facing. Romans 12:1–2 talks about presenting our bodies as living sacrifices and about not conforming to the pattern of this world. These are tough things for a young person to grasp. But Paul goes on to say that by this "we test and approve what God's will is—his good, pleasing and perfect will" (NIV). When we instruct our children, we show them that the way we propose is the best thing for them. Not only is it "good," it is "pleasing and perfect."

Nourish

There is one more word used in Ephesians 6:4 that we need to look at. Fathers are told to "bring them up in the discipline and instruction of the Lord." "Bring them up" is from a word (*ektrephō*) that means "to nourish or nurture." This has the idea of "to raise a child to maturity providing for physical and psychological needs."[6] Children should know that their fathers are there for them whatever happens; that they are fully committed to their nourishment and will do whatever it takes to accomplish it. Parents do not only advise, instruct, and discipline. Their children should know that the parents are there to support them when they have a crisis or are under attack. They should know that the parents are totally committed to do what is best for their welfare. Generally, people associate such care and concern as coming from mothers. But it is significant that Paul's instruction in Ephesians is given to fathers.

Praying is a good way to nourish children. The Bible presents prayer as a work that we do for others (see Col. 4:12–13; James 5:16). Children should know that their fathers pray for them daily, and that when they have some need, the father, not only the mother, is going to pray for it. When my children were living at home and I was on a journey abroad, if the children had some crisis, they would tell their mother to inform me. They knew that I would pray about it. This was before the days of mobile phones. These days, they inform me directly. When a concerned father knows that a child is having a physical, spiritual, or emotional problem, he calls home often to find out how the child is doing. This is a way of expressing solidarity with the child in his or her situation.

If the daughter is getting ready to leave home for an exam and finds that she does not have something she needs, such as a pen or an eraser, the father volunteers to rush to the shop and get one. If a son is about to leave for a party and realizes his shoes need polishing because he has just been walking through mud, the father quickly shines them. These are all actions that come from a desire to provide for the child. Of course, they are also features of a happy home.

Respond Consistently

Consistency in responding to stressful situations is an important aspect of discipline. It helps children to develop a proper attitude to right and wrong and gives them an atmosphere where respect can be fostered. Both of these are very important for the healthy growth of a child.

Agree about Discipline

Catherine Booth was the very capable wife of William Booth, the founder of the Salvation Army. Both she and her husband were highly opinionated people, but they had a happy and fruitful marriage. Before their wedding, Catherine set four rules that she hoped would govern their relationship. They were: (1) never have secrets; (2) never have separate purses; (3) talk out differences to secure harmony rather than pretend differences don't exist; and (4) never argue in front of the children.[7] Mrs. Booth's fourth rule is particularly important when it comes to disciplining children. Children are not mature enough to know how to handle the sight of parents arguing in front of them. A stray comment that implicates a child may result in the child thinking that he is responsible for the disagreement between the parents. Thereafter, whenever his parents fight, he may think that he is the cause.

But more seriously, when parents disagree about discipline in front of a child, it reduces the child's respect for the discipline. A child can be crafty and pit one parent against the other. Suppose a father expresses displeasure in front of his son over the harshness with which the mother disciplined him. The next time the father comes home from work, the son may complain to the father about something the mother did to discipline him. If the father responds again by rebuking the mother, the result is that the boy loses his respect for his mother and for the whole idea of discipline. This will cause serious damage to his healthy growth.

Stand Firm

Here is a common scenario: a small girl asks for something and the mother refuses. The child begins to scream, demanding that she get it. The mother, unable to handle the strain of listening to her daughter screaming, gives in and gets what the child wants.

The child learns that if she screams loud enough and long enough, she can get things that her mother does not want to give her. This sends a message to the child. It says: "Ultimately, my mother gives me things not based on whether it is right or wrong, but based on her comfort and convenience. If I can make my mother really uncomfortable, I can get a lot of things that she doesn't want to give me."

The Bible teaches that we should not need to swear because we should really mean what we say. James says, "But above all, my brothers, do not swear, either by heaven or by earth or by any other oath, but let your 'yes' be yes and your 'no' be no" (James 5:12; see also Matt. 5:33–37). Just as God is faithful and consistent in all his ways, his followers also are to be consistent. Children learn that from their parents.

But there is another important message that is communicated by a mother's refusal to wilt when the child screams. When the mother remains firm, her daughter learns that there will be times in her life when she will not get what she wants. This is certainly a reality in adult life. If children do not learn to be content in the midst of "no" experiences in life, they are going to be unhappy people. Life brings with it many things we do not like and many desires that we cannot fulfill. Parents have a great responsibility to train their children to graciously accept "no" experiences. One of the best ways to do that is to be consistent with their yes and their no.

Foster Attitudes of Respect

Parents' consistent responses to the stubborn insistence of children also help them foster attitudes of respect in their children. Dobson says:

> There are times a strong-willed child will clench his fists and dare his parents to accept his challenges. He is not motivated by frustration or inner hostility, as is often supposed. He merely

wants to know where the boundaries lie and who's available to enforce them. Many well-meaning specialists have waved the banner of tolerance, but offered no solution for defiance. They have stressed the importance of parental understanding of the child, and I concur. But we have to teach children that they have a few things to learn about their parents, too![8]

Respecting those to whom respect is due is a very important value in the Bible. One of the consequences of parents disciplining consistently is that the children respect their parents. Hebrews 12:9 says, "Moreover, we have all had human fathers who disciplined us and we respected them for it" (NIV). The first four of the Ten Commandments deal with our relationship with God. The next six have to do with our relationships with people, and the first of those relates to honoring parents: "Honor your father and your mother, that your days may be long in the land that the LORD your God is giving you" (Ex. 20:12). Paul describes this as "the first commandment with a promise" (Eph. 6:2). Learning to respect parents, then, is a key aspect of the healthy growth of a child.

From learning to respect their parents, children learn that respect is an important value in life. From that, they learn to respect others. Paul teaches: "Pay to all what is owed to them: . . . respect to whom respect is owed, honor to whom honor is owed" (Rom. 13:7). The Bible tells believers to respect (1 Thess. 5:12), remember the example of (Heb. 13:7), and obey and submit to (Heb. 13:17) Christian leaders. Several times, Paul exhorts employees to submit to secular bosses or employers (Eph. 6:5; Col. 3:22; 1 Tim. 6:1; Titus 2:9). Peter goes so far as to say, "Servants, be subject to your masters with all respect, not only to the good and gentle but also to the unjust" (1 Pet. 2:18). Clearly, respecting people in authority is a key Christian trait.

Sadly, this value is rapidly disappearing from society. Often, if a teacher disciplines a child or if a coach drops a child from a team, parents rise up in strong protest. The result is that teachers' hands are tied, and they are unable to discipline children. Indeed, there are extreme cases that may need parental intervention. But parents should weigh the options carefully before doing this, as respect for teachers is something they should be helping to foster in their children.

A similar thing happens in churches. A parent keeps complaining to the child about the Sunday school or the youth fellowship he attends, saying, "This is not the way we did it," "Why are you not memorizing Scripture? That's something we did when we were in Sunday school," or "We were taught discipline in Sunday school." Ironically, that statement about discipline could undermine the discipline of the children. If children know that their parents do not respect their youth leaders and Sunday school teachers, they also may not respect them. Then they may refuse to submit to those leaders or teachers. They can hide behind their parents' attitudes and refuse to submit to the necessary disciplines of the group. The result will be stunted growth.

If parents want to criticize the Sunday school or the youth fellowship, they should tell the leaders of these groups or the leaders of the church, such as the pastor. They should not involve the children. Criticizing in the way I described could be a sign of insecurity of the parents. They may be reluctant to hand over their children to others, wanting to keep control of the children exclusively to themselves. They are threatened when someone who is different influences their children. The end result could be that these children ultimately rebel against such control by the parents.

For Their Welfare, Not Our Name

The final point I want to make about discipline is that all discipline and instruction given to children is primarily for their welfare, not because their parents are leaders in the church. The fact that the parents are humiliated by the action of a child is a secondary matter. Children may resent their parents' involvement in church leadership if they are asked to do or not to do things only because their parents are in ministry. We adults were the ones who responded to the call to ministry, not our children. Our spouses, in a sense, responded to the call because they chose to marry those of us in ministry. Our children did not choose to be born into ministry families. Making such statements as "What will people think?" or "That is not the way a Christian leader's child behaves" is not a good way to motivate children to holiness. Insensitive and immature church members may say things like this to the children of leaders. That is unfortunate. But that must not be the driving factor in our pushing some course of action for our children.

We ask our children to pray and read their Bibles every day because that is good for them, not because they are children of Christian leaders. That is our will for all the children in the community to which we belong—not only the children of leaders. Every child needs to be holy. If we prohibit our children from going to some place or event, it is because it is not good for them, not because the children of Christian leaders should not be seen in such places. People often murmur against the behavior of the children of Christian leaders. If the charge is true, the children need to be rebuked and perhaps disciplined. But the children must be left with the impression that the discipline was because of their wrong acts and for their welfare, not because people talked about their behavior.

I also need to say that our children should not be given special treatment in their Christian group because we are among the leaders. The idea of the "crown prince" with special privileges has no place in Christian community living. Both my children are in their thirties and continue to be enthusiastically involved in Youth for Christ, one as a full-time staff member and the other as a volunteer. But they were not given special treatment in their youth. Sometimes I spoke at camps where they were among the campers. Often, the other campers did not know that they were my children. Sometimes they instructed my wife and me not to talk with them (and we were delighted when they came and talked to us).

My wife and I were very happy when my son felt that God was

calling him to ministry in Youth for Christ. But we did not encourage him too much in this. We wanted him to receive conviction of a clear call from God without us pushing it. So when he finished his software engineer's degree and told us that he still wanted to join YFC, we asked him first to do a job. After a year of working, he told us that he had no doubt that he was called, and we gave him the freedom to pursue that call.

Conclusion

The point that has come out over and over again in this chapter is that we must conscientiously practice biblical principles in the raising of our children. It is an important task, but it is not an easy one. Often we are tempted to act in ways that are not in keeping with the biblical lifestyle. So we must think hard and talk through issues with our spouses so that we will act in ways that are honoring to God and helpful to our children.

13

Instructing Children

Earlier, I quoted the nineteenth-century Presbyterian pastor-theologian Robert Dabney, who said, "The education of children for God is the most important business done on earth."[1] The home is the primary place where children are taught the most important things in life. Large portions of the book of Proverbs, especially in chapters 1 to 9, are related to parents teaching their children and the children's response.

We cannot expect comprehensive instruction about the way to live to come from schools, most of which now focus on the curriculum required for progressing academically and give little encouragement to the pursuit of Christian values. For example, Western culture is not going to teach our children that extramarital sex is wrong. Sadly, many churches are not emphasizing that teaching either. This is possibly because many young people are involved in extramarital relations, so churches are afraid that young adults will be uneasy and perhaps leave the church if they talk against it. Not surprisingly, surveys are showing that many young-adult children of evangelicals in the West have given up the biblical view of sex: that it should be confined to a relationship between a man and a woman within marriage. The influence of the culture has been greater than the influence of the home and the church. This points to an urgent need for parents to instruct their children on the Christian ethic.

Instruction in the home is done in several ways. We will look at some of these ways in this chapter.

Instruction through Life

Chip Ingram, in his excellent book *Effective Parenting in a Defective World*, says: "Character is always more caught than taught. Always."[2] I do not know whether there is biblical support for that assertion. While often talking about the importance of examples, the Bible also says a lot about the power of words to change people's character. I prefer to say that character is caught *and* taught.

Nevertheless, there is strong biblical support for the power of example in molding character. Paul says, "Be imitators of me, as I am of Christ" (1 Cor. 11:1). He makes similar assertions at least five times (1 Cor. 4:16; 10:33; Phil. 3:17; 1 Thess. 1:6; 2 Thess. 3:9). He tells his spiritual child, Timothy, "You, however, have followed my teaching, my conduct, my aim in life, my faith, my patience, my love, my steadfastness, my persecutions and sufferings" (2 Tim 3:10–11). Donald Guthrie shows that the word translated as "followed" (*parakoloutheō*) carries the idea of "to trace out as an example."[3] Paul's life was an open book to Timothy, and he had learned by observation how Paul would act in different situations.

Children's deep-seated views about God are greatly influenced by the behavior of their parents. Using the example of a mother's love, Isaiah teaches about the unrelenting caring of God, but shows that it far supersedes the caring of a mother: "Can a woman forget her nursing child, that she should have no compassion on the son of her womb? Even these may forget, yet I will not forget you" (Isa. 49:15). While this example is given to contrast God's love with that of an unfaithful mother, it also implies that a faithful mother can give a child a picture of the nature of God.

A mother goes through discomfort for nine months and then a painful delivery to enable her child to enter this world. During the child's nine months in the womb, and then during the first few months after the birth, she produces nourishment from her own body for the child. Even after that, she is responsible for giving the child the best nourishment. She stays up caring for the child during times of sickness with what looks like supernatural perseverance and infinite sacrifice. All this illustrates God's provision for our needs, climaxing in Christ's death for our salvation. The love of a mother for her rebellious child gives us a picture of a God whose persistent love for his rebellious creation caused him to send his own Son for our salvation.[4]

Fathers are presented as an example of God's compassion: "As a father shows compassion to his children, so the LORD shows compassion to those who fear him" (Ps. 103:13). They are also shown as exemplifying God's faithfulness in responding to our needs: "If you then, who are evil, know how to give good gifts to your children, how much more will your Father who is in heaven give good things to those who ask him!" (Matt. 7:11). Here the emphasis is on how much more reliable God is. But Jesus's teaching here does show that fathers should illustrate God's reliability by their behavior. One who has not experienced such love and consistent faithfulness from his or her parents will find it difficult to believe that God loves him and cares for him through all the experiences of life. Sadly, I must say that I have seen this in the lives of many people whose parents (or one of them) proved to be unreliable or deeply disappointed them. It is very difficult for them to believe that God will look after them.

Children learn a lot from their parents by observation. They intuitively take the behavior of their parents as acceptable and do the same. D. L. Moody tells the story of a mother who, surprised by the ringing of the doorbell, whirled around to see who was there and broke a tumbler in the process. When she came back to the kitchen, she found that her young daughter, thinking that breaking tumblers was the right thing, had broken all that she could get her hands on.[5] In Sri Lanka, parents often tell lies to their children for short-term gain. They may instruct a child to tell an unwelcome visitor that they are not at home. They may say that some terrible person, such as "the bogeyman," will come and take them away if they do not eat their food properly. When the father leaves home on a long journey and the child cries over his departure, to stop his crying, the mother may tell him that his father has gone to the shops and will be back soon. Soon he realizes that his parents (whom he sees as devout Christians) lie often in order to achieve various ends, and he assumes that it is acceptable for Christians to lie.

The Christian ethic is so different from the ethic followed by many in the culture in which we live. Our children are going to be exposed heavily to that ethic through their personal contacts and through the media. The common idea is that living according to the principles of Christianity is not practical in this world. Parents can demonstrate the falseness of that idea by living principled lives. Or, by their example, they can communicate to their children that Christian ethics are not practicable.

A family in India went on a long journey by train, and the father was able to get very good seats by paying a bribe and jumping the queue. When the son questioned this action, the father said, "Oh, everybody does it." When it came time for that son to go to university, the father was able to get him into a prestigious school by paying another a bribe. When the son questioned the propriety of this action, the father replied, "Everybody does it." Later, the parents were shocked when that son was dismissed from the university for cheating on an exam. When the sad parents asked, "Son, why did you do it?" he replied, "Everybody does it."

When Parents Fail
Children can reject Christianity when they see their Christian parents breaking Christian principles. That is a very serious thing!

Jesus said, "It would be better for him if a millstone were hung around his neck and he were cast into the sea than that he should cause one of these little ones to sin" (Luke 17:2).

Many of today's Christian leaders came to Christ in their youth, an age of rebellion against the status quo. They saw the status quo as hypocritical or inauthentic and became open to authentic Christianity. These people rebelled against what appeared to them to be the inauthentic lives of their parents and found that Christianity offered them an authentic life. Embracing vibrant Christianity was a consequence of their rejection of their parents' religious traditions. Now these people have become leaders and their children have become youth. It is these young people's turn to rebel against the status quo. For them, rebelling against the status quo means rebelling against Christianity. Christian parents therefore must do all they can to demonstrate to their children that Christianity is an authentic faith.

Some children who see their actively Christian parents breaking Christian principles become what we might call "cultural Christians." These are people who consider Christianity to be part of their social identity and the church to be the institution that nurtures that identity. The church is very important to them. They are involved in the church and may hold positions in the church. But like their parents, they do not follow the principles taught in the Bible.

This is a very dangerous situation. The church is harmed when influential members do not follow the principles that are a basic aspect of life in the church. It is also very dangerous for these cultural Christians. Being in the church, they know the principles of Christianity, but they do not follow them. Jesus describes the fate of such people in these chilling words: "That servant who knew his master's will but did not get ready or act according to his will, will receive a severe beating. But the one who did not know, and did what deserved a beating, will receive a light beating. Everyone to whom much was given, of him much will be required, and from him to whom they entrusted much, they will demand the more" (Luke 12:47–48).

I must also say that I have met several children of Christian leaders who, while being very upset by the failure of their parents to follow Christian principles at home, nevertheless decided that they would seek to be sincere followers of Christ. In those cases, the influence of grace was greater than the influence of their Christian parents' inconsistency.

Yet the fact remains that we all fall short of God's principles. James 3:2, referring to teachers, says, "For we all stumble in many ways." Much of the damage from these errors can be avoided if we accept that we have done wrong and apologize to our family members. We talked about this in chapter 9. We said that when a family member, especially a parent, does wrong, a cloud of heaviness hangs in the air in that home. The others in the family are disappointed, angry, unhappy, or uneasy about the behavior of the wrongdoer. When children become youth and start questioning anything that sounds inauthentic, they may question the authenticity of the faith of a parent who professes to be Christian but refuses to acknowledge his or her sin. Acknowledging sin, of course, is a basic practice in the Christian life. When the family member admits that he or she has done wrong and apologizes, the cloud is cleared.

When my children were small, if I was under a lot of pressure at work, I would sometimes snap at them unreasonably. When I did this, I knew that I must apologize to them. But I would find many excuses to avoid this humiliating step! I would reason that it was good for the children to face such situations, as they were going to face this kind of unreasonable behavior when they went out into the world. But I knew my reasons were not genuinely acceptable. I knew I must go to them and apologize. Even though apologizing is humiliating to parents, I believe they win the respect of their children when they do so. By contrast, they forfeit their spiritual authority by their refusal to accept their wrongdoing.

Perhaps they maintain an outward peace, with the children treating them with respect because they have to. But they have lost their credibility. God is dishonored by their sin, and this dishonor is compounded by their refusal to confess their wrongs.

When Christian parents apologize to their spouses and their children, they teach the children that wrongdoing should be confronted honestly and responsibility for it accepted. They also uphold the holiness of God by refusing to condone their own unholy behavior. Apologizing, therefore, should be a regular practice in a Christian home.

Instruction through Teaching

One of the most important passages in the Bible about the response to the Word of God by God's people is Deuteronomy 4. Several points there spell out what the people were to do with the Word. In the middle of this passage, there are two instructions about parents communicating the Word and the works of God to their children. Deuteronomy 4:9 says, "Make [God's works on your behalf] known to your children and your children's children." In the next verse, Moses quotes God as saying, "Gather the people to me, that I may let them hear my words, so that they may learn to fear me all the days that they live on the earth, and that they may teach their children so." These words show parents are to teach the works and the Word of God to their children. In the Bible, parents are the most important teachers of the Word to God's people. They hear God's Word so that they can learn to fear the Lord and teach their children.

Proverbs 1:8 gives a good summary of parents' influence on their children: "Hear, my son, your father's instruction, and forsake not your mother's teaching." Perhaps we should not make too much of the difference between the "teaching" of the mother and the "instruction" of the father. This is typical of the parallelism that characterizes Hebrew poetry—two statements meaning almost the same thing. But it is significant that the word translated as "teaching" is the common word *torah*, the word given to the first five books of the Bible by the Israelites. Used here, it surely has the sense of teaching the content of the Scriptures. The word used for the father's role, translated as "instruction," has the idea of "discipline, correction, training, exhortation, and warning," which emphasizes applying the Scriptures. Again, with the caution that we should not make too much of a distinction, we can say that children need both to be taught the content of the Scriptures and to be instructed in applying it to day-to-day life. Often, mothers are the ones who find the time to do systematic teaching, and fathers are more adept at applying the truth of Scripture to the challenges that children face in life. These roles, of course, can be interchanged. But we must not forget that fathers also have an important role in teaching the children. The book of Proverbs points this out often (e.g. Prov. 1:8; 4:1; 6:20; 13:1; 15:5).

The classic text on teaching the Word to children is Deuteronomy 6:6–9:

> And these words that I command you today shall be on your heart. You shall teach them diligently to your children, and shall talk of them when you sit in your house, and when you walk by the way, and when you lie down, and when you rise. You shall bind them as a sign on your hand, and they shall be as frontlets between your eyes. You shall write them on the doorposts of your house and on your gates.

Each statement in this text has important affirmations that we will consider, as well as looking more closely at Deuteronomy 4.

Teach the Word

Parents are told to "teach [God's Word] diligently to your children" (Deut. 6:7a). In the Hebrew, "teach . . . diligently" is one word meaning "to repeat." The advertising industry has grasped the importance of repetition in helping children acquire a message. The *Houston Chronicle* reported: "Researchers in San Diego monitored ninety-five hours of weekday afternoon and Saturday morning television shows targeted at children. The two-month study revealed children are exposed to twenty-one commercials an hour."[6] This is a case of persistent and repetitive instruction. It fits more closely with the model of teaching described as being primarily done by the mother.

I like to think of myself as being a Bible teacher. I learned the art of biblical interpretation and teaching from reading the books (from my layman father's library) of some world-renowned writers, such as John Stott, F. F. Bruce, and Leon Morris, and from being taught by several wonderful seminary teachers, including Robert Traina, Daniel Fuller, Donald Demaray, Robert Coleman, John Oswalt, and Joseph Wang. But as far as the contents of Scripture and my attitude to the Bible are concerned, the most influential teacher in my life was my mother. She would wake her children most mornings, get us together, and go through the Bible with us. She covered both the Old and New Testaments.

My mother came to Christ from Buddhism in her teens. As far as I know, she never took a class on how to study the Bible. But she knew the Word and she taught it to us. All her five children are committed Christians serving God in lay or full-time capacities. Following her example, my wife taught the Scriptures to our children. She first used *The Picture Bible* published by David C. Cook,[7] which is in comic-book style and covers most of the stories and teachings of the Bible. She went through the whole book about twice with each child. When the children could read, they also went through the book on their own. Just as this teaching of my mother had a huge impact on me, I regard my wife's influence on my children as the most important human factor in their commitment to Christ and to Christian ministry.

Talk about the Word[8]

The next affirmation in Deuteronomy 6 is about talking about the Word: "Talk of [God's Word] when you sit in your house, and when you walk by the way, and when you lie down, and when you rise" (6:b7). The picture here is constant input into the lives of children.

Different aspects of family life are mentioned. Parents are to talk about the Word when they "sit in [their] house." Mealtime in the home is ideal for such conversation. Usually there is an atmosphere of informality and warmth during mealtime that is well suited to foster discussion. Some of the happiest times in the life of a family are at the dinner table, when they talk about the things that matter most in life.

Next, parents are commanded to teach their children the Word of God "when [they] walk by the way." In many cultures today, "walking by the way" would need to be revised to "driving in the family vehicle." Travel time provides a good opportunity for lively conversation.

Finally, parents are told to talk about the Word "when [they] lie down, and when [they] rise." They need to help children think about God at the start and the end of the day. That will help them to be godly all through the day. By doing this, we affirm that all of life is under God's lordship and that he is with us. Therefore, we do not need to fear, because God will look after us. We often disobey because we lose our trust in God to see us through a situation. The messages of the world overcome the influence of the Word of God. The best way to counteract this is to be constantly exposed to the Word. In Old Testament times, when the people were not bombarded through the media with the unbiblical messages we receive today, so much more time was spent discussing the Word than today. Considering the volume and content of what we are exposed to today, we should be spending more time with the Word than the people in Old Testament times so as to counteract the anti-Christian messages that we encounter! Clearly this is an area that needs urgent attention.

So the Word is to be the topic of discussion in ordinary conversation. This can happen through what I might call Word-directed testimony, in which we talk about what we have learned from the

Bible, perhaps in our devotions or through a message we heard. Then we can discuss passages we find difficult to understand. We can share difficult issues we face and see what the Word has to say about them. When we see a movie, a TV program, or an advertisement, we can evaluate it using criteria from the Word as our benchmark. Because we seek to be Word-directed in everything we do, we discuss what the Word has to say about each situation we face. How important this is for children, who are bombarded by so many anti-Christian thoughts through the media and through their regular contacts. They are told that it is OK to be selfish and to progress by hurting others; it is OK to lie; it is OK to pay bribes; it is OK to hate those of another race; it is OK to enjoy sexual relations outside marriage; and it is OK to pursue happiness through luxuries and status. This presents a huge challenge to parents. As I said in the last chapter, parents need to study the issues facing their children in order to give them Word-directed guidance on how to respond.

Sadly, family discussion has gone out of vogue in today's world. Writing in 1970 in an article entitled "The High Price of TV," Joseph Bayly quotes Dr. Graham Blaine, the chief psychiatrist in the student health service at Harvard University, as saying that "the most serious problem of TV is not poor programming, but that it has destroyed the average family's exchange of views and information at the evening meal. People are anxious to get to their favorite program, . . . so they hurry to finish eating." Bayly adds, "What happened during the day, the little things, and bigger matters are never discussed."[9] Now, with smartphones and their access to the Internet, this problem has been aggravated greatly. Often, when a family goes out for a meal at a restaurant, the children and sometimes the parents spend the time working away on their phones.

Yet in today's world, the Internet has provided a meaningful way of conversation for a lot of people, as is shown by the use of the word *chat* for Internet communication. I know that my son has good discussions on vital issues with his friends by chatting over the Internet. Both my children have asked me questions over the Internet, which has provided me with thrilling opportunities to enter into serious discussions with them. Sometimes my children are in the next room, but they still find the Internet to be a meaningful medium for chatting with me.

Lift High the Word

In addition to the topics mentioned above, Deuteronomy 4 says that it is important to teach children about God's acts on behalf of his people. This is emphasized several times in the Bible, especially in Deuteronomy. One of the acts that is often mentioned is the miraculous way in which God gave the Word to the people (vv. 10–13). Moses describes how the people "came near and stood at the foot of the mountain, while the mountain burned with fire to the heart of heaven, wrapped in darkness, cloud, and gloom" (v. 11). Then he says that "the LORD spoke to you out of the midst of the fire. You heard the sound of words, but saw no form; there was only a voice" (v. 12). There are eleven references in Deuteronomy to God speaking his Word "out of the fire" (4:12, 15, 33, 36; 5:4, 22, 23, 24, 26; 9:10; 10:4). Given this repetition, it must be important. It means that God authenticated the revelation he was giving in miraculous ways so that the people would know that the truth being communicated was absolutely unique. Similarly, the events surrounding Jesus's birth, life, teaching, death, resurrection, and ascension authenticate the absolute uniqueness of the words of the apostles and their representatives who wrote the New Testament.[10]

In our pluralistic world, the idea of absolute truth that guides our behavior sounds strange to most people. Pluralists affirm that absolute truth is unknowable. If there is an absolute God, he cannot be known fully, though different peoples have experienced some truth about him. So there is a cultural trend against taking the teachings of the Bible as absolutely essential for life. Many biblical teachings go against the grain of what a lot of people are thinking. Many people are repelled by the idea that faith in Christ is the only way to salvation. They don't like the biblical belief that sexual relations should be confined to a married male and female. Sadly, many younger Christians seem to have wilted under the strain of this strong current of opinion.

One way this moral and doctrinal slide can be avoided is by nurturing in youth a strong sense of the absolutely binding authority of the Word of God. If they know that the Bible indeed comes directly from the almighty God, who is Lord of the whole universe, then they have a strong compulsion to obey what it says and to believe that what it says is needed for the whole world. In other words, they need to be convinced that the Bible is absolute truth—in the sense that it is necessary for everyone. So we must show our children that the Bible is indeed the Word of the living God, that he inspired it as no other book has been inspired. That will challenge them to take it seriously.

In my youth, it was not unusual to find preachers in my denomination who said that many of the stories in the Bible were not historical. They said that the Bible was not completely inspired by God and therefore contained errors. My mother often warned us about the danger these ideas posed. I am thankful that I never really departed from the approach to Scripture that my mother taught us. In my early twenties, I was a theological student in the United States of America when evangelical theologians were battling over the inspiration of the Bible. There I read a book by J. I. Packer titled *"Fundamentalism" and the Word of God*,[11] which showed me that belief in the trustworthiness of Scripture has an intellectually credible base. It was my mother's insistence on the trustworthiness of Scripture that helped lay the foundation for my later convictions on the nature of the Bible. Packer helped me develop an intellectual case for that belief.

Non-Westernized youth may not be so powerfully impacted by postmodern thinking. But they face the challenge of cultures that generally respect the scriptures of their religions but do not think it is necessary to practice what they teach. The majority of the people in Sri Lanka affirm the scriptural statement of their religion that they should not lie. But lying is very much a part of our culture. The parents of non-Westernized Christian youth also have the huge challenge of convincing their children that the Christian Bible is a book like no other that must be obeyed in day-to-day life.

Relate the Story of Salvation

Deuteronomy 4 also teaches that parents should tell their children about God's marvelous acts on their behalf and of their salvation from slavery. Moses says: "Only take care, and keep your soul diligently, lest you forget the things that your eyes have seen, and lest they depart from your heart all the days of your life. Make them known to your children and your children's children" (v. 9). The history of Israel was unique, and it molded the identity of the Israelites. Moses goes on to say, "Has any god ever attempted to go and take a nation for himself from the midst of another nation, by trials, by signs, by wonders, and by war, by a mighty hand and an outstretched arm, and by great deeds of terror, all of which the LORD your God did for you in Egypt before your eyes?" (v. 34). Their deliverance came because they were a chosen people for whom God had a plan. This election was an important part of their identity. Moses says, "He loved your fathers and chose their offspring after them and brought you out of Egypt with his own presence, by his great power, driving out before you nations greater and mightier than you, to bring you in, to give you their land for an inheritance, as it is this day" (vv. 37–38).

Every Christian family has a story to tell about the marvelous grace of God to them. Some can see how grace has been passed down through a Christian heritage that goes back many generations. Others found God's grace only recently after previous generations had lived in darkness. But all can rejoice in their history of God's gracious intervention in their lives. Parents must tell this to their children. The psalmist says, "We will not hide them from their children, but tell to the coming generation the glorious deeds of the LORD, and his might, and the wonders that he has done" (Ps. 78:4).

Children learn truths best through stories. An important time in the life of any Christian family is when they recount the stories of God's dealings with their family members and others. Stories of conversion, of answers to prayer, and of challenges overcome by God's power form part of family lore. This can be shared during family devotions, at the dinner table, or during conversation around a bed or elsewhere. Conversation about experiences the family has had can become a very strong identity-buttressing tool in the life of the children. They should have a sense that, "This is our history; this is who we are; and it is beautiful." This will help them when they grow up and are tempted to do things that contradict the principles that are part of the Christian heritage of their family. The power of their identity as part of a Christian family that follows God will serve as a deterrent to acting in ways that violate their identity. Often, when prodigals who have gone astray return to God, they say that they just could not shake off the influence of their Christian heritage, which was so much a part of their identity.

Use Visual Aids[12]

After asking parents to teach the Word and talk about it (Deut. 6:6–7), Moses goes on to recommend the use of visual aids to remind children and adults about the contents of Scripture. First, he talks of armbands and headbands: "You shall bind them as a sign on your hand, and they shall be as frontlets between your eyes" (v. 8). Then he talks about inscriptions at the entrance to house and property: "You shall write them on the doorposts of your house and on your gates" (v. 9). This type of thing was regularly practiced in the ancient Near East. Israel's neighbors used these methods in superstitious ways, just as people use good-luck charms and talismans today. But God directed his people to use them as reminders of their covenant identity and their covenant responsibility to obey God's Word.

It is interesting how the Bible invests holy meanings into practices that people of other faiths used for their religious rituals, redeeming them to be used for God's glory. Today, we are sometimes afraid to do this because of the pagan connotations attached to some practices. Indeed, we must be careful when we venture into these areas. But many practices are not bad in themselves, such as having a band around your wrist. It is the use of wristbands in superstitious ways that is problematic. The Bible says we should have such a passion to communicate God's truth that we may use any means that can break through to people's hearts, so long as it does not harm the receiver of the message.

When I was child, my grandmother kept a painting on the wall of her house. It depicted a bunch of red roses and the words "Kept by the Power of God. 1 Peter 1:5" (this is the King James Version). I have never forgotten that. In fact, the first sermon I preached, when I was still a teenager, was on that verse. The church has several symbolic items that have been derived directly from the Scriptures—such as the Lord's Supper and baptism. To these we could add symbolic items that help us remember the Word of God. Calligraphy with Scripture verses on our walls was common at one time. I was encouraged when young people began to wear bands with the letters WWJD, from the motto "What would Jesus do?" While things like this can become meaningless fads, I believe many use them out of a sincere desire to be obedient to God.

While what is prescribed in Deuteronomy 6 has to do with remembering the words of God's law, visual and sensory aids were also prescribed to help the people remember key events in Israel's history. After the people crossed the River Jordan, God asked Joshua to tell the people to take twelve stones out of the riverbed and carry them to the place where they camped that day. Joshua said the stones would be "a sign among you" (Josh. 4:6a). Then he said, "When your children ask in time to come, 'What do those stones mean to you?'" they were to tell the children the story of the crossing of the Jordan (vv. 6b–7).

In the same way, rituals during Israel's annual festivals were to remind the people of key features of the events being celebrated. A. W. Morton explains: "Through participation in the festivals, the children would learn their meaning, and in this way the festivals became a part of life indelibly etched upon their minds. The festivals were unique opportunities for teaching the young the great truths of the Jewish faith. They provided a dramatic, vivid and intrinsically interesting way of teaching."[13] Bitter herbs were eaten during the Passover to symbolize the bitterness of the slavery from which the people were delivered (Ex. 1:14; 12:8; Num. 9:11). Unleavened bread, which was bread prepared in haste, was also eaten at the Passover to remind the people of their hurried exit from Egypt and also of the pilgrim character of their lives (Ex. 12:11, 20, 34, 39). With the other festivals, however, there were celebratory special meals. Today, special meals at Christmas can remind people of the good news of great joy that came through the birth of Christ.

Conclusion

The people of God in the Bible took pains to systematically and creatively communicate biblical truth to children. We should do the same. This will help buttress the identity of children as belonging to God's people, and help the truth of God go deep into their beings. This will make it much more difficult for them to permanently remain rebellious to God when they are adults. Proverbs puts it well: "Train up a child in the way he should go; even when he is old he will not depart from it" (Prov. 22:6).

Conclusion

I want to conclude this book with a few affirmations, each accompanied by a charge. They are general affirmations that apply to all of life, but they are very appropriate to family life.

Affirmation: God is greater than every challenge we face in life, including those in family life.
Charge: Believe God, refuse to give up hope, and strive with utmost dedication for healing and resolution.

Affirmation: God's love is greater than all the pain we experience.
Charge: Stay close to God and receive his love, which heals and strengthens you and brings joy to your life.

Affirmation: God's way is the best way for doing everything.
Charge: Study his Word and conscientiously practice it in your home life.

Affirmation: God never calls without giving us the enabling to fulfill the call.
Charge: Take hold of his enabling by faith and obedience.

Now to him who is able to do far more abundantly
than all that we ask or think, according to
the power at work within us, to him be glory
in the church and in Christ Jesus throughout
all generations, forever and ever. Amen.

Ephesians 3:20–21

Notes

Preface

1. Andreas J. Köstenberger with David W. Jones, *God, Marriage, and Family: Rebuilding the Biblical Foundation*, 2nd ed. (Wheaton, IL: Crossway, 2010). The book that I used at first was the earlier edition.

Chapter One: God

1. Rodney "Gypsy" Smith, "How a Husband Was Converted," in *The Methodist Message* (Singapore), April 1909; repr., March 2011, 4.
2. Dwight Lyman Moody, "Address to Parents," in *Classic Sermons on Family and Home*, ed. Warren W. Wiersbe (Peabody, MA: Hendrickson, 1993), 73.
3. Ibid., 77–78.

Chapter Two: Crucifying Self

1. This point is made by F. F. Bruce in *Romans: An Introduction and Commentary*, Tyndale New Testament Commentaries (Downers Grove, IL: InterVarsity Press, and Nottingham, UK: Inter-Varsity Press, 1985), 223.
2. This story was related to me by my friend, the founding chairman of the Missions Department at Wheaton College, the late Dr. John Gration.

Chapter Three: Love

1. I explained many points in this and the next two sections in greater detail in my book *Reclaiming Love* (Grand Rapids, MI: Zondervan, 2013).
2. H. Norman Wright, *Premarital Counseling* (Chicago: Moody Press, 1981), 122.

Chapter Four: God's Beautiful Plan

1. Warren W. Wiersbe, *The Bible Exposition Commentary*, vol. 2 (Wheaton, IL: Victor Books, 1996), 142.
2. Andreas J. Köstenberger with David W. Jones, *God, Marriage, and Family: Rebuilding the Biblical Foundation*, 2nd ed. (Wheaton, IL: Crossway, 2010), 59.

3. Emerson Eggerichs, *Love and Respect: The Love She Most Desires; the Respect He Desperately Needs* (Nashville: Thomas Nelson, 2004), 19.

Chapter Five: Sexual Love

1. Philip Graham Ryken, *Written in Stone: The Ten Commandments and Today's Moral Crisis* (Wheaton, IL: Crossway, 2003), 157.
2. Ibid.
3. Terry Fisher, quoted in Michael Medved, *Hollywood vs. America* (New York: HarperCollins, 1992), 111–112, quoted in Ryken, *Written in Stone*, 157.
4. Sharmila Mandre, in "Bangalore Times," *The Times of India*, March 25, 2007.
5. C. J. Mahaney, *Sex, Romance, and the Glory of God: What Every Christian Husband Needs to Know* (Wheaton, IL: Crossway, 2004), 10.
6. Bruce K. Waltke, *The Book of Proverbs: Chapters 1–15*, The New International Commentary on the Old Testament (Grand Rapids, MI, and Cambridge, UK: Eerdmans, 2004), 320.
7. Matthew uses a slightly different but closely related word.
8. Leon Morris, *The Gospel According to Matthew*, The Pillar New Testament Commentary (Grand Rapids, MI: Eerdmans; Leicester, England: Inter-Varsity Press, 1992), 481.
9. See the numerous articles at www.christianitytoday.com under the search topics "women" and "lust."
10. Willard F. Harley Jr., *His Needs, Her Needs: Building an Affair Proof Marriage* (Grand Rapids, MI: Revell, 2001), 49.
11. H. Norman Wright, *Premarital Counseling* (Chicago: Moody Press, 1981), 124.
12. Many years ago, I read an article in *Themelios*, a journal for theological students, that cited research in this area that had been done at a university in Arizona.
13. Daniel Heimbach, *True Sexual Morality: Recovering Biblical Standards for a Culture in Crisis* (Wheaton, IL: Crossway, 2004), 181 (italics added).
14. Much of the material in this section is adapted from my booklet *Sensible Behaviour: How to Avoid Indiscreet Relationships* (Colombo, Sri Lanka: Youth for Christ Publications and several publishers in other countries, 2007).
15. Jay Kesler, *Being Holy, Being Human* (Carol Stream, IL: Christianity Today Inc., and Waco, TX: Word Books, 1988), 142.
16. Ibid., 143.

Chapter Six: Joy

1. These figures are from H. van Broekhoven Jr., "Joy," in *International Standard Bible Encyclopedia*, vol. 3, ed. Geoffrey Bromiley et al (Grand Rapids, MI, and Cambridge, UK: Eerdmans, 1982), 1142–43.

2. Though the ESV uses the word *blessed*, I found several versions that use *happy*.
3. Tim Stafford, *Never Mind the Joneses: Building Core Christian Values in a Way That Fits your Family* (Downers Grove, IL: InterVarsity Press, 2004), 152.
4. Tim Stafford, quoted in Marshall Shelley, *The Healthy Hectic Home: Raising a Family in the Midst of Ministry* (Carol Stream, IL: Christianity Today, Inc., and Dallas, TX: Word Publishing, 1988), 30–31.
5. C. S. Lewis, *Reflections on the Psalms* (New York: Harcourt, Brace & World, 1958), 95.

Chapter Seven: Disappointment and Pain

1. We do not know much about the character of Jehoiahaz, another of Josiah's sons who reigned for just three months.
2. *Reclaiming Love* (Grand Rapids, MI: Zondervan, 2013), chaps. 3, 4, 5, and 17.
3. These points have been gleaned from the following sources: Mark A. Noll, "Benjamin Warfield," *Handbook of Evangelical Theologians*, ed. Walter A. Elwell (Grand Rapids, MI: Baker, 1993), 27; Fred G. Zaspel, *The Theology of B. B. Warfield: A Systematic Summary* (Wheaton, IL: Crossway, 2010), 29–30; and Fred G. Zaspel, "Annie Pearce Kinkead (Mrs. B. B.) Warfield," *Credo Magazine* blog, http://www.credomag.com /2013/04/24/annie-pearce-kinkead-mrs-b-b-warfield/, accessed April 13, 2015.
4. Mark Noll, "The Struggle for Lincoln's Soul," in *Books and Culture*, vol. 1, no. 1, September/October 1995, 3–5; quoted in John Piper: *A Godward Life* (Sisters, OR: Multnomah, 1997), 34.
5. Lyle Dorsett, *A Passion for God: The Spiritual Journey of A. W. Tozer* (Chicago: Moody Press, 2008), 106–8.
6. Quoted in ibid., 160.
7. I have expounded on these themes in a fuller way in my book *The Call to Joy and Pain: Embracing Suffering in Your Ministry* (Wheaton, IL: Crossway, 2007).
8. Paul Tournier, *Creative Suffering* (London: SCM Press, 1982), 60.
9. Leon Morris, *The Epistle to the Romans*, The Pillar New Testament Commentary (Grand Rapids, MI: Eerdmans; Leicester, England: Inter-Varsity Press, 1988), 325.
10. Paul Sangster, *Dr. Sangster* (London: Epworth Press, 1962), 54; cited in Warren W. Wiersbe and Lloyd M. Perry, *The Wycliffe Handbook of Preaching and Preachers* (Chicago: Moody Press, 1984), 217.
11. P. E. Sangster, "Foreword," in W. E. Sangster, *Westminster Sermons, Vol. 2: At Fast and Festival* (London: Epworth Press, 1961), n.p.
12. Noll, "The Struggle for Lincoln's Soul," 3, quoted in Piper, *A Godward Life*, 34.
13. Ibid.

14. A. T. Robertson, *A Grammar of the Greek New Testament in the Light of Historical Research* (London, n.d.), 573.
15. Taken almost verbatim from Kenneth W. Osbeck, *Amazing Grace: 366 Inspiring Hymn Stories for Daily Devotions* (Grand Rapids, MI: Kregel Publications, 1996), 193.
16. From the hymn "No One Ever Cared for Me Like Jesus" by Charles F. Weigle. Copyright © 1932 New Spring Publishing (ASCAP) (adm. at EMICMGPublishing.com). All rights reserved. Used by permission.
17. *Reclaiming Love.*
18. David A. Seamands, *Healing for Damaged Emotions* (Wheaton, IL: Victor Books, 1981), 30–31.
19. Ruth Bell Graham, *Prodigals and Those Who Love Them* (Colorado Springs, CO: Focus on the Family Publishing, 1991), 100. The excerpts are drawn from John 17:11–24 (KJV).
20. Isaiah Hoogendyk, ed., *Lexham Analytical Lexicon to the Septuagint* (Bellingham, WA: Lexham Press, 2012–2014), in Logos Bible Software.

Chapter Eight: Unity

1. Quoted in Cindy and Steve Wright, "Finishing Well—Ruth and Billy Graham—Marriage Message #309," Marriage Missions International, http://marriagemissions.com/finishing-well-ruth-and-billy-graham-finishing-well-marriage-message-309/, accessed May 20, 2015.
2. Chuck and Barb Snyder, *Incompatibility: Still Grounds for a Great Marriage* (Sisters OR: Multnomah Publishers, 1999).
3. I read this in the *Asbury Seminary Herald* magazine about thirty-five years ago.
4. H. Norman Wright, *Premarital Counseling* (Chicago: Moody Press, 1981), 104–5.
5. W. Arndt, F. W. Danker, and W. Bauer, *A Greek-English Lexicon of the New Testament and Other Early Christian Literature*, 3rd ed. (Chicago: University of Chicago Press, 2000), 939.

Chapter Nine: The Love Fight

1. The title of this chapter, "The Love Fight," is borrowed from the subtitle of a book by David Augsburger, *Caring Enough to Confront: The Love-Fight* (Glendale, CA: Regal Books, 1976). The original title of this book was *The Love-Fight*.
2. Sandra D. Wilson, *Hurt People Hurt People: Hope and Healing for Yourself and Your Relationships* (Nashville: Thomas Nelson, 1993).

Chapter Ten: Delighting in Children

1. Quoted in Kent and Barbara Hughes, *The Disciplines of a Godly Family* (Wheaton, IL: Crossway, 2004), 16.
2. Ibid.
3. William Holladay, *A Concise Hebrew and Aramaic Lexicon of the Old Testament* (Leiden: Brill, 2000), 59.

4. Warren W. Wiersbe, *The Bible Exposition Commentary*, vol. 2 (Wheaton, IL: Victor Books, 1996), 54.
5. Johannes P. Louw and Eugene A. Nida, *Greek-English Lexicon of the New Testament*, 2nd ed., vol. 1 (New York: United Bible Societies, 1989), 461.
6. This story is related with some differences in detail in my book *Reclaiming Love* (Grand Rapids, MI: Zondervan, 2013), 70–71. While the story is fictional, it combines some incidents from my life with a few other points.
7. Victor R. Fuchs, *Women's Quest for Economic Equality* (Cambridge, MA: Harvard University Press, 1988), 111; cited in Dorothy Kelley Patterson and Armour Patterson, *A Handbook for Parents in Ministry* (Nashville: Broadman & Holman, 2004), 111.
8. Ibid., 63.
9. Based on personal conversation and correspondence with Dr. Lalith Mendis.
10. Louw and Nida, *Greek-English Lexicon of the New Testament*, 809.

Chapter Eleven: Fun, Traditions, and Security for Children

1. G. F. Hasel, "Games," *International Standard Bible Encyclopedia*, vol. 2, ed. Geoffrey Bromiley et al (Grand Rapids, MI, and Cambridge, UK: Eerdmans, 1982), 398.
2. Chip Ingram, *Effective Parenting in a Defective World* (Carol Stream, IL: Tyndale, 2006), 33.
3. See Raymond Villanueva, "The Positive and Negative Effects of Cartoons on Children's Behavior," Prezi, https://prezi.com/467gmsuzlv-k /the-positive-and-negative-effects-of-cartoon-on-childrens-behavior/, and Novak Djokovic "Negative Impacts of Cartoons," Novak Djokovic Foundation, http://blog.novakdjokovicfoundation.org/education /negative-impacts-of-cartoons/, both accessed July 3, 2015.
4. See John Trent, Rick Osborne, Kurt Bruner, eds., *Parent's Guide to the Spiritual Growth of Children* (Carol Stream, IL: Tyndale, 2000), 311–312, 390–391.
5. I am grateful to my youth worker son Asiri for this information.
6. Tim Stafford, *Never Mind the Joneses: Building Core Christian Values in a Way That Fits Your Family* (Downers Grove, IL: InterVarsity Press, 2004), 155.
7. "Festival," *Dictionary of Biblical Imagery*, ed. Leland Ryken et al (Downers Grove, IL: InterVarsity Press, 2000), 281.
8. Ibid., 282.
9. John Wesley, *Explanatory Notes upon the Old Testament*, vol. 1 (Bristol: William Pine, 1765), 248; on Ex. 15:1.
10. Quoted in Paul Lee Tan, *Encyclopedia of 7700 Illustrations: Signs of the Times* (Garland, TX: Bible Communications, 1996), 679.
11. Stafford, *Never Mind the Joneses*, 155.

12. Johannes P. Louw and Eugene A. Nida, *Greek-English Lexicon of the New Testament*, 2nd ed., vol. 1 (New York: United Bible Societies, 1989), 293.
13. Leon Morris, *1 and 2 Thessalonians: An Introduction and Commentary*, Tyndale New Testament Commentaries (Downers Grove, IL: InterVarsity Press, and Nottingham, UK: Inter-Varsity Press, 1984), 58.
14. David A. Seamands, *Healing for Damaged Emotions* (Wheaton, IL: Victor Books, 1981), 97.

Chapter Twelve: Disciplining Children
1. Warren W. Wiersbe, *The Bible Exposition Commentary*, vol. 2. (Wheaton, IL: Victor Books, 1996), 54.
2. James C. Dobson, *The New Dare to Discipline* (Wheaton, IL: Tyndale, 1992), 5.
3. Johannes P. Louw and Eugene A. Nida, *Greek-English Lexicon of the New Testament*, 2nd ed., vol. 1 (New York United Bible Societies, 1989), 466.
4. See James Dobson, *Hide or Seek* (Old Tappan, NJ: Revell, 1974), 81–88.
5. Louw and Nida, *Greek-English Lexicon of the New Testament*, 414.
6. Ibid., 463.
7. Marshall Shelley, *The Healthy Hectic Home: Raising a Family in the Midst of Ministry* (Carol Stream, IL: Christianity Today Inc., and Dallas, TX: Word, 1988), 15.
8. Dobson, *The New Dare to Discipline*, 5–6.

Chapter Thirteen: Instructing Children
1. Quoted in Kent and Barbara Hughes, *The Disciplines of a Godly Family* (Wheaton, IL: Crossway, 2004), 16.
2. Chip Ingram *Effective Parenting in a Defective World* (Carol Stream, IL: Tyndale, 2006), 15.
3. Donald Guthrie, *The Pastoral Epistles: An Introduction and Commentary*, Tyndale New Testament Commentaries (Downers Grove, IL: InterVarsity Press, and Nottingham, UK: Inter-Varsity Press, 1990), 178.
4. See Dennis F. Kinlaw, *The Family: Sacred Pedagogy* (Wilmore, KY: The Francis Asbury Society, n.d.).
5. Dwight Lyman Moody, "Address to Parents," in *Classic Sermons on Family and Home*, ed. Warren W. Wiersbe (Peabody, MA: Hendrickson, 1993), 74.
6. *Houston Chronicle*, June 22, 1995, 5D.
7. Iva Hoth and Andre Le Blanc, *The Picture Bible* (Colorado Springs: Cook, 1998).
8. Much of the material in this section is adapted from my *Deuteronomy: Loving Obedience to a Loving God*, Preaching the Word (Wheaton, IL: Crossway, 2012), 263–67.

9. Joseph T. Bayly, *Out of My Mind: The Best of Joe Bayly*, ed. Timothy Bayly (Grand Rapids, MI: Zondervan, 1993), 101. The wording here is Bayly's.

10. I have argued for the absolute uniqueness and authority of the words of Jesus using John 14:6–11 in *The Supremacy of Christ* (Wheaton, IL: Crossway, 1995; London: Hodder and Stoughton, 1997; Secundarabad: OM Books, 2005).

11. J. I. Packer, *"Fundamentalism" and the Word of God* (Grand Rapids, MI, and Cambridge, UK: Eerdmans, 1958).

12. Some of the material in this section is adapted from my *Deuteronomy: Loving Obedience to a Loving God*, 268.

13. A. W. Morton, "Education in Biblical Times," *The Zondervan Encyclopedia of the Bible*, vol. 2 (Grand Rapids, MI: Zondervan, 2009), 242.

General Index

Scripture Index